From Cradle to Retirement

The Child IRA

Also by Christopher Carosa...

Hey! What's My Number?

 – How to Improve the Odds You Will Retire in Comfort

A Pizza The Action

 – Everything I Ever Learned About Business I Learned by Working in a Pizza Stand at the Erie County Fair

50 Hidden Gems of Greater Western New York

 – A Handbook for Those Too Proud to Believe "Wide Right" and "No Goal" Define Us

401(k) Fiduciary Solutions

 – Expert Guidance for 401(k) Plan Sponsors on How to Effectively and Safely Manage Plan Compliance and Investments by Sharing the Fiduciary Burden with Experienced Professionals

Due Diligence

 – The Individual Trustee's Guide to Selecting and Monitoring a Professional Money Manager

From Cradle to Retirement

The Child IRA

How to Start a Newborn Baby
on the Road to Comfortable Retirement
While Still in a Cozy Cradle

by

Christopher Carosa

Pandamensional Solutions, Inc.

Mendon, New York

Published by Pandamensional Solutions, Inc., Mendon, NY

Cover design by Catarina Lena Carosa

ISBN-10: 1-938465-05-9
ISBN-13: 978-1-938465-05-5

From *FiduciaryNews.com* Articles:

"The Child IRA is a common sense solution and should be part of the bigger approach to fixing our retirement system. Congress must consider this and work out the tax structure aspect so future generations have money, sustainable for retirement. These are the kinds of ideas that I think young working Americans can get excited about. It helps them be "for" something rather than worry about something they inherently feel will not be there for them when they reach retirement age. I think there is still much to be worked out with the Child IRA idea but it is a start and I fully endorse new solutions to America's retirement crisis, not the same old, same old." (August 18, 2015)

➤ Congressman Tom Marino, 10th District, Pennsylvania

"The Child IRA could be an incredibly powerful tool for combatting not only the looming retirement crisis, but also the long-term care burden that my and future generations are likely to face as our parents get older. When it comes to compound interest, the longer your investing horizon, the less you have to contribute to achieve outstanding results. Mathematically, starting to save for retirement as a newborn could drastically reduce the savings burden in your working years. Not to mention it would likely do an enormous favor to the child from a financial literacy perspective. I absolutely plan to take advantage of this when my husband and I have children. Obviously, not every child is cut out to be a model, but as you mention in your articles, there are other ways for children to earn enough income as they get older to catch up. For example, I've been working since I started babysitting at eleven years old. I wish I had known enough to take advantage of a Child IRA." (November 15, 2016)

➤ Tara Falcone, CEO, Founder, ReisUP

For my future grandchildren:
I hope your parents read this book and remember it.

TABLE OF CONTENTS

Section One: Overview

Section Two: From the Lens of History

Section Three: The Child IRA Basics

Section Four: The Practical Child IRA

Section Five: The Child IRA – Your Next Step

Section Six: Appendices

FOREWORD

With apologies to Karl Marx, George Santayana, Oscar Wilde, Plato and the Campbell Soup Company, should history repeat itself, hopefully your legacy won't include missing this "middle class millionaire" opportunity.[1]

In this "read all about it" book, complete with suggestions and case studies, Chris Carosa shouts the opportunity available to all Americans that they can leave a rich legacy for their children and grandchildren.

If Chris Carosa was evaluated using the GREGORC Style Delineator™, I bet he would score out the same as myself – a "practical dreamer." Chris and I certainly share admiration for founding father Ben Franklin. *From Cradle to Retirement*, Chris shares the entertaining story of Ben Franklin's long term (200 year) investment decision. He reconfirms and reminds us that Ben Franklin believed in and was confident about America's future.

Franklin's works were designed to improve the public. Franklin's optimism rested on the possibilities open to individual Americans – what we often call "the American Dream." Revolutionary in his day, the essence of Franklin's dream was that any man can earn prosperity, economic security, and community respect through hard work and honest dealings with others. Franklin preached that the possibilities were limitless. Franklin shaped American expectations – that the lowliest citizen was as humanly worthy as the wealthiest because of his potential for earning wealth and that poverty was disgraceful only if one failed to do something about it.

In large part due to Franklin, "the American Dream" is a national ethos of Americans, a set of ideals (equality, liberty, rights, democracy) including the opportunity for prosperity and success, as well as an upward social mobility for the family and children to be achieved through hard work in a society with few barriers. One definition is "that dream of a land in which life should be better and richer and fuller for everyone, with opportunity for each according to ability or achievement" regardless of social class or circumstances of birth.[2]

I also believe striving for "the American Dream" is liberating – "financial security is the ultimate civil liberty."[3] Even if you have despaired about achieving "the American Dream" yourself, what if history repeats itself? If it does, the Child IRA may be your children's (and grandchildren's) best opportunity.

Observational learning is often the most effective method of education. Through his actions, Franklin's vision of America's future challenges us: What will we teach our children and grandchildren? What legacy will we leave? If you are a parent, you too have confidence in America's future. You obviously believe in making the small, necessary, day to day sacrifices as a parent – however – your natural selflessness means parenting really isn't a sacrifice but a reward. I can confirm that opening and maintaining a Child IRA will also be a rewarding experience – for you and your child.

Ben Franklin would agree that the Child IRA can be part of a legacy rich in love, confidence, imagination, determination, resilience, discipline, independence, hope and, if history repeats itself, … riches. Such a legacy is only strengthened where the child contributes her own earnings – learning the values of work, saving, and financial prudence. This family legacy is one that can be renewed and refreshed with every successive generation.

In 2017, some revile America's historical figures – they cover statues of Thomas Jefferson with shrouds or they deface memorials to Francis Scott Key and Abraham Lincoln. Certainly, Ben Franklin had many flaws. He was a slave owner. He was a common man at birth – but uncommonly wise and optimistic. His legacy of making long term investments in future American generations, unknown to him, reconfirms the rich legacy we have inherited as Americans.

It is your turn.

Jack Towarnicky
Executive Director
Plan Sponsor Council of America
Columbus, Ohio

ACKNOWLEDGEMENTS

How do you thank the many people that allow you to pursue your passion? Do you start with your parents and grandparents, whose faithful loyalty gave you the desire for and the presence of an ultimate destiny to help others? Do you include your siblings, who, despite the required bickering, never shied from paving the way (often in ways they'll never realize)? Do you list all your nieces, nephews, aunts, uncles, and extended family for always taking an interest in and actively listening to your latest exploits? Do you go through a long list of life-long friends, business associates, and enthusiastic supporters?

In the case of *From Cradle to Retirement*, I must start with my children – Cesidia, Catarina, and Peter. Children have this great ability to lend perspective on things. They help you realize and understand things that you wouldn't otherwise see so easily. We all live with the regret "if only I knew then what I know now." In your children, you can actively recreate that "if only," not for your advantage, but for their advantage.

As a mature adult, you can look back and connect your dots. As a parent, you can help your children look forward to connecting their dots. Of course, you don't want to go overboard. On one hand, you don't want to push your child to take the road you didn't take just because you always wanted to know what would have happened. Likewise, you don't necessarily want to push your child away from the wrong road you took just because you don't want them to suffer as you once did. (After all, a little suffering benefits us all.) Finally, you have to contend with "I'm not going to do it, but only because you told me to do it."

Now, there are some things you can do as a parent that don't require your children to understand or even agree to. This was precisely the case when I started Child IRAs for my children. They were old enough to "get" the idea of saving and investing, but they weren't particularly interested in keeping an eye on things – at least until they were a lot older (it turns out many of the parents I interviewed had similar experiences). My only regret is "if only I had known what I know now" when my kids were babies!

Beyond the need to furtively allow my children to benefit from my experience, this book owes itself to many people who have encouraged my writing throughout the years. Caroline Marwitz and Paul Wilson, my editors at *BenefitsPro*, were among the first to see and publish the very beginnings of the Child IRA concept. Many other reporters and media outlets have since picked up on the idea (news flash, the Child IRA is not the same IRA for teenagers you've been seeing since the advent of the IRA). One reporter in particular, Sarah O'Brien from CNBC, asked a great question. Although my answer didn't make her report, it did make it in *From Cradle to Retirement* (see my Introduction that follows this section).

There have been quite a few financial professionals who have taken a liking to the Child IRA concept, but none more than Jack Towarnicky. Jack has been busy making sure the idea gets in front of people and organizations that can most benefit others by spreading the word of the Child IRA.

Finally, I would be remiss if I didn't thank both my daughter Catarina, who did a really fine job with the book cover (yes, she drew the picture on the front cover), and my wife Betsy, Jennifer Crowley, and Stephen Ranelli, all who caught all the typos I made in the manuscript (but not the ones I made after she proofed the pages). Of course, I also need to thank all the "babies" (with one exception, they're all adults now and the other one seems like he's an adult) – Teresa, Pat, Cesidia, Catarina, Peter, Sam, and Joey!

Christopher Carosa
Mendon, New York
March 12, 2018

INTRODUCTION:
MY PASSION EXPLAINED

I was too young to do anything about it then, but I'll never forget that helplessness. I've always thought, "If only I could have done something..." Now I can.

I remember growing up in the shadows of the gargantuan steel mill complex. At its peak, it employed 30,000 people, including the parents, grandparents, and other family members of many of my elementary school classmates. But then the world changed. Suddenly, the dozens of smoke stacks stopped belching. The steel plant was gone. And with it, thousands and thousands of jobs, thousands and thousands of hopes, thousands and thousands of dreams.

To me, those many thousands weren't merely faceless statistics, but the very human community that touched my young life every day. Each one of these good, kind, caring neighbors believed in the promise of the establishment that controlled their lives. When the factory shut its doors that final time, so too did those institutions. The company failed them. The union failed them. The government failed them. They lost everything – their jobs, their retirement plan, and, unfortunately, sometimes even more.

Worse, we lost our community. As families moved away in search of jobs, the once bustling six lane highway that fed into the heart of the plant now had an eerie resemblance to the main street of an abandoned ghost town. The rusting remnants of the aging rolling mills, coke ovens, and blast furnaces tormented those brave enough to remain with the taunting memories of what once was.

I watched this sad drama unfold. I was too young to do anything about it then. But I never forgot the helplessness. Though I lamented, "If only I could do something…," I vowed to forever strive to come up with some idea that would prevent innocent people from ever again falling victim to those large institutions who, despite good intentions, will never see them as anything more than faceless statistics.

Today's headlines predict further harm to those who continue to rely on the kindness of strangers

We've seen headlines predicting the coming insolvency of Social Security. Quite simply, this government run safety net is spending more money than it's taking in. Officials predict the Social Security Trust Fund will be depleted in 2034 ("A Summary of the 2017 Annual Reports," Social Security and Medicare Boards of Trustees, July 2017). Furthermore, the reports do not predict the situation will resolve itself, and its projections extend 70 years to nearly the end of this century.

The happy accident of discovery

In the intervening years, and especially in the last decade, I've interviewed hundreds of people involved in the retirement industry – from people saving for retirement to retirement plan service providers to state and government regulators. These interviews have produced hundreds of stories, articles, and reports published for national audiences by print and digital media outlets. As a result of this experience, my thoughts and opinions have been sought out and broadcast on various national TV and radio networks. But it wasn't until I made a mistake on a spreadsheet I used in one of my previous books (*Hey! What's My Number? How to Increase the Odds You Will Retire in Comfort*, Pandamensional Solutions, Inc, 2014) that I accidentally discovered an incredibly easy solution to better prepare Americans for retirement without relying on the kindness of government, their employer, or any other stranger. That's when I discovered The Child IRA.

It happened while preparing a graphic I often used when teaching Boy Scouts the Personal Management merit badge. This merit badge, which every Eagle Scout must earn, contains a section that explains "the time value of money," or "compound interest" as many call it. I would demonstrate this through two characters: Early Earl and Late Larry. Early Earl was – you guessed it – the same age as the typical Boy Scout I'd teach. He'd begin saving $1,000 a year at age 15 and continue through age 30. Late Larry would also save for sixteen years, only he would start, well, later. At age 40. And to make up for his tardiness, he'd save five times more - $5,000 a year. Despite saving this greater amount, by the time they retire, Early Earl's savings would have grown 50% more than Late Larry's. That's the power of compound interest.

Now, as I was running through my numbers prior to the publication of *Hey! What's My Number?* I accidently entered a "0" for the age Early Earl would start saving. Naturally, I quickly caught the error and fixed it, but not before curiosity caused me to explore the idea of beginning to save immediately after being born. That little trek created a new character – "Turbo Tot." Compared to Early Earl and Late Larry, Turbo Tot's savings grew astronomically, ending at age 70 with almost three times more than Early Earl's total and into the "multi-millionaire" range. In the subsequent articles I wrote about this discovery, I labeled Turbo Tot's savings plan "The Child IRA."

If there were a way for every newborn child to retire a multi-millionaire, wouldn't every parent want to know it?

The concept is quite simple. From the moment the baby is born, you save $1,000 a year in a Child IRA until the baby's 19th birthday. Then you do nothing. If that money is invested for the long-term and earns 8% (which is 3% less than the average 11% long-term return for stocks), then, when that child retires at age 70, the Child IRA account would have grown to two-and-a-quarter million dollars.

Alas, there's a catch. There is no such thing as a "Child IRA." In reality, parents who create a Child IRA today must establish a traditional IRA, but there are restrictions which limit whether a child qualifies. Don't you think parents want to know what they could do right now to allow their child to benefit from a Child IRA?

I think so.

From Cradle to Retirement pieces together the thoughts and interviews I've accumulated over the past several years to reveal a practical "How-to" guide for parents, grandparents, and their financial advisers seeking to help young children reap the benefits of the Child IRA. Within this hands-on guide, *From Cradle to Retirement* weaves the fascinating history of the cultural views of retirement in America and the implications these have had on public policy. Finally, and perhaps of greatest interest, *From Cradle to Retirement* reveals real-world case-studies of people who have created actual Child IRAs for their children. Still more case-studies show how parents have attempted to duplicate some of the Child IRA's features with other savings vehicles.

Speaking of those case-studies…

SECTION ONE:

– OVERVIEW –

SOME FEAR THE FUTURE,
OTHERS CAPITALIZE ON THE FUTURE,
WHICH DESCRIBES YOU?

CHAPTER ONE:
HOW A CASUAL BREAKFAST WITH HIS FATHER CHANGED HIS CHILDREN'S LIVES FOREVER

Todd Erkis pulled into the Bob Evans parking lot, his father riding shotgun as he had so many times before. "Breakfast with Dad" had become a favorite ritual for the two. Little did Todd know, but on this warm summer morning in August 2000 his father would reveal to him an idea that would change his children's lives forever.

After graduating from Westerville North High School in 1982, Todd left his hometown of Columbus, Ohio to attend the University of Pennsylvania. Located just outside of Philadelphia, he earned a Bachelor's Degree in economics from the Wharton School. Following the completion of his undergraduate studies in 1986, he began his career as an actuary, eventually becoming Chief Actuary of Lincoln Financial. Today, Todd Erkis is a professor of finance and risk management at Saint Joseph's University in Philadelphia. He's also the author of the book *What Insurance Companies Don't Want You to Know: An Insider Shows You How to Win at Insurance*. Despite this solid background in finance and economics, it was Todd's father Ron, an orthodontist in Ohio's capital city, that would ultimately reveal the idea that could leave Todd's children hundreds of thousands of dollars wealthier than they might otherwise be.

"My father and I spoke often about finance and he was a big influence in my life when it came to saving and investing," says Todd. "My father started talking about Roth IRAs. I was working at that time as an actuarial consultant at PricewaterhouseCoopers (PwC) so I was familiar with the concept of a Roth." Working for a large financial services firm, Todd read the *Wall Street Journal* regularly, so he was able to quickly understand the potential long-term benefits of the suggestion his father made to him that morning as they ate their oatmeal and biscuits at their favorite eatery.

Todd tells the story like this: "My father is an orthodontist who recently stopped working full-time but is still working part-time. He had a very successful practice and for many years has attended financial seminars run by Collier and Associates. I am not totally sure if it was in a newsletter or at one of the seminars but the idea of employing working age children in the practice and using the earnings to start a Roth IRA was discussed. Roth IRAs were new at that time and his suggestion of possibly starting one for my kids sounded good to me."

Edwina and Todd Erkis have three children, a girl and two boys. Their oldest, a daughter, was born in 1990. "She was very mature for her age and at age 10 made money here and there by walking people's dogs and being a 'mommy's helper'," recalls Todd. "I started to keep track of everything she earned (it was no more than a few $100) and started the Roth IRA for her in 2000 when she was 10. The regular annual deposits started at age 14 when she started babysitting more, lifeguarding, and giving swimming lessons, and continued until she had access to a 401k at her work. I did a similar thing for my two boys as well (now ages 24 and 22). Each of them has a good deal of money in their accounts invested in the S&P 500 which will hopefully grow to quite a sum when they are of retirement age 40 - 45 years from now."

Indeed, since Todd started these IRAs for his children, the investment returns alone have already doubled the value of those funds. Imagine that kind of modest growth steadily accumulating in those accounts over the decades as Todd's children progress in their careers. Each child plans to continue saving for their retirement through corporate plans, just like many other adults. But it is these IRAs their father started for them when they were children that can make a difference between merely a comfortable retirement and a more comfortable retirement. This supplemental retirement savings shows the power of compound earnings. "When they retire, it will have grown to be in the hundreds of thousands of dollars," says Todd. "The key is starting early so the money can grow tax free for a long time."

The Erkis' represent just one of a number of families who have discovered the broad benefits of starting IRAs for their children. Not only do these vehicles enhance a child's prospects at retirement, but they also teach them early on the value of saving, planning, and self-responsibility.

From Cradle to Retirement, while briefly exploring the historic attitudes of America regarding retirement policy, focuses on explaining the concept of The Child IRA. Through real-life case studies, what you are about to read demonstrates how families are today establishing IRAs for their minor children. The book contains interviews with people within industries that regularly employ minor children – including newborn babies (hint: think "advertising") – to give parents some idea as to what their children might do to establish a Child IRA. It even shows how to "catch-up" if you didn't start a Child IRA the first year your child was born (including what needs to be done if you start as late as college graduation). Finally, *From Cradle to Retirement* addresses what types of policy changes might make The Child IRA more accessible to a greater number of families – and how it might just save Social Security. Imagine if the Child IRA could combine the power of compounding found in a 401k plan with the flexible contributions allowed by a 529 plan!

In the next few pages, you'll discover:

- Why Americans, originally borne of these traits, may have lost them over the past century or so.
- An easy-to-understand explanation detailing how a newborn baby today, without any changes in the law, can become a multimillionaire by the time of retirement – all with just a $1,000 contribution every year for 19 years into a Child IRA.
- How other families have realized and implemented child-based savings strategies similar, if not identical to the one employed by the Erkis family.

- How financial service providers have created practical non-IRA based savings strategies for children and real-life examples of these strategies you can easily duplicate.
- What changes in retirement policies and legislation need to occur for The Child IRA to become more broadly available to potentially every child in America (and how to enact these changes with no cost to the federal budget).

Who knows? Perhaps reading this book will forever change the lives of your children, grandchildren, nieces and nephews, too. I know of at least one Founding Father who was thinking not just about the political future of America's future generations, but their financial future, too. We'll explore this surprisingly overlooked advice next.

CHAPTER TWO:
A PIECE OF BEN FRANKLIN'S WISDOM
YOU MAY NOT KNOW

Who remembers these quotes? "A penny saved is a penny earned." "Early to bed and early to rise makes a man healthy, wealthy and wise." "Time is money." "Never leave until tomorrow that which you can do today." "God helps those who help themselves."

Of all our nation's Founding Fathers, perhaps none was more a rascal than Ben Franklin. That goes without saying because, unlike his fellow rebel elite, Franklin stands alone as the scientist of the group. As we all know, from Galileo to Feynman, scientists make the greatest pranksters. Indeed, if Groucho Marx hadn't been born to a Vaudevillian family, he, too, might have challenged Einstein at the Pantheon of early twentieth century scientists.

Benjamin Franklin was born January 17, 1706 on Milk Street in Boston, Massachusetts. His father, Josiah Franklin made soap and candles. Benjamin was one of fifteen children born to Josiah in his two marriages and was his tenth and last son. His parents couldn't afford to send him to school, so young Ben's formal education ended at age ten. After spending a couple of years working for his father, his brother James took him on as an apprentice in his printing company.

Imagine being the youngest son in that era. You got pushed around and everywhere you turned someone was wagging their finger at you saying, "You can't do that!" If you wanted to get anywhere you had to be diligent, persistent, and, well, wily creative. Ben demonstrated all that. When his brother James refused to print Ben's letters in the newspaper he published, Ben figured out a way around this obstacle. He created a make-believe middle-aged widow called "Silence Dogood" (in today's Facebook era, we'd call this a "Fake Account") and got his letters published under this pseudonym. You might remember the name "Silence Dogood" as it's a critical element in the plot of the popular Nicolas Cage movie *National Treasure*.

Silence Dogood represented the tip of the iceberg in the brothers' relationship. "Ben and his brother never got along particularly well, and after several years of learning the printing trade, Ben managed to wriggle out of his apprenticeship and set off on his own," says David S. Rose, author of Angel Investing and The Startup Checklist and CEO of Gust in New York City. "While most apprentices of the time simply became journeymen, and continued working for other people, Franklin, as an entrepreneur, decided at a very young age to set up his own business."

At age 17, Ben ran away to Philadelphia, Pennsylvania and into the history books. Indeed, Dr. Whitfield Bell Jr., at the time executive officer of the American Philosophical Society and well-studied in the lore of Franklin, told the story of a Philadelphia physician who once publicly corrected Oliver Wendell Holmes, immediately after Holmes had just noted Franklin was born in Boston, saying that "Franklin was born in Philadelphia at the age of 17."[1]

But it's not the precise definition of Ben's "birth" nor his oft-told life story that concerns us. Rather, it is his death. More precisely, the will he had created that was executed following his passing. "I have been a Frankophile most of my life," says Jack Towarnicky, Executive Director at Plan Sponsor Council of America in Columbus, Ohio. "I am a sucker for combinations of common sense (cents) and innovation. My GREGORC™ mind style is 'practical dreamer,' so, when my brother-in-law Ron Goldwyn and my sister Carol, longtime Philadelphia residents, shared the story of Ben Franklin's Last Will and Testament, I was immediately hooked."

The origin of the Benjamin Franklin Trusts (Philadelphia and Boston each had one) bears remembering. Franklin would become the first notable American to wear the cloak of the rogue scientist. His science is without question, most famously in the episode involving a kite, a key, and a random stroke of lightning. He combined both his scientific method of thinking with his playful mischief-maker attitude when he stunned the Paris court by debunking the popular Franz Mesmer's mysterious cure.

Asked by King Louis the Sixteenth and Marie Antoinette to serve on a committee to test Mesmer's mind-altering methods, Franklin quickly concluded Mesmer's techniques had nothing to do with the claims of the patients. It was all in the patients' minds. To prove this, Franklin blindfolded the patients and asked Mesmer to perform his magic. Fearing the inevitable, Mesmer sent an assistant. The blindfolded patients still believed they could feel the "mesmerization" (yes, this is where we get the word), even though it wasn't being applied.[2]

Ben Franklin wasn't just good at dishing it out, he was equally adept at taking it. When French Mathematician Charles-Joseph Mathon de la Cour decided to spoof Franklin's *Poor Richard's Almanack* with the parody Fortunate Richard, Franklin was up to the task. Mathon de la Cour wanted to make fun of Frankln's famous optimism. He kiddingly suggested "Fortunate Richard" leave a small sum in his will with instructions not to distribute it for 500 years. After those five centuries, it would have grown considerably, the largesse enough to pay for the most extravagant of desires.[3]

Franklin wasn't insulted. In fact, he thanked Mathon de la Cour and proceeded to draft such a codicil in his own will, the only difference being the duration of the trust – Franklin's was to last only 200 years. Yet, despite the appearance of playfulness in his response, Franklin treated the matter with cold scientific calculus. In doing so, he showed us an important lesson.

Ben Franklin died on April 17, 1790. He left a large estate but a much larger philosophy. Here reads a portion of his last will and testament:

"I have considered that, among artisans, good apprentices are most likely to make good citizens, and, having myself been bred to a manual art, printing, in my native town, and afterwards assisted to set up my business in Philadelphia by kind loans of money from two friends there, which was the foundation of my fortune, and all the utility in life that may be ascribed to me, I wish to be useful even after my death, if possible, in forming and advancing other young men, that may be serviceable to their country in both these towns. To this end, I devote two thousand pounds sterling, of which I give one thousand thereof to the inhabitants of the town of Boston, in Massachusetts, and the other thousand to the inhabitants of the city of Philadelphia, in trust, to and for the uses, intents, and purposes herein after mentioned and declared."[4]

Franklin then laid out precisely how he wanted the trusts managed. He wanted the money to go to young people who, like himself, sought to begin their lives learning a trade. These loans would charge 5% interest. To be eligible, applicants must be:

"such young married artificers, under the age of twenty-five years, as have served an apprenticeship in the said town, and faithfully fulfilled the duties required in their indentures, so as to obtain a good moral character from at least two respectable citizens, who are willing to become their sureties, in a bond with the applicants, for the repayment of the moneys so lent, with interest, according to the terms hereinafter prescribed."[5]

"Ben Franklin was the quintessential American entrepreneur," says Rose. "Unlike all the other Founding Fathers, Franklin viewed himself first and foremost as a businessman, and fervently believed that public servants should not be paid. In fact, the 2,000 pounds that he left in his will for the establishment of the funds came from his salary as Governor of Pennsylvania. He therefore established the two funds in his will expressly for the purpose of lending start-up funds to young men who had completed their apprenticeship so that they could create their own businesses. The funds were not for education, not for apprenticeship programs, not for scholarships, not for institutions… they were designed to help kickstart entrepreneurial tradesmen like himself!"

Franklin was not merely an advocate of entrepreneurism, he was also one heck of a financier. His will actually calculated the precise growth he expected from the trusts and further instructed the trustees in terms of allocating those assets at the end of the first hundred years and again at the end of the second hundred years upon which the trust would be terminated. These instructions, in the actual words of Ben Franklin, were:

> "If this plan is executed, and succeeds as projected without interruption for one hundred years, the sum will then be one hundred and thirty-one thousand pounds; of which I would have the managers of the donation to the town of Boston then lay out, at their discretion, one hundred thousand pounds in public works, which may be judged of most general utility to the inhabitants, such as fortifications, bridges, aqueducts, public buildings, baths, pavements, or whatever may make living in the town more convenient to its people, and render it more agreeable to strangers resorting thither for health or a temporary residence. The remaining thirty-one thousand pounds I would have continued to be let out on interest, in the manner above directed, for another hundred years, as I hope it will have been found that the institution has had a good effect on the conduct of youth, and been of service to many worthy characters and useful citizens. At the end of this second term, if no unfortunate accident has prevented the operation, the sum will be four millions and sixty one thousand pounds sterling, of which I leave one million sixty one thousand pounds to the disposition of the inhabitants of the town of Boston, and three millions to the disposition of the government of the state, not presuming to carry my views farther."[6]

Now, for those not familiar with late-eighteenth century currency exchange rates on the impact of inflation during the 200+ years since Franklin's death, those gifts of £1,000 in 1790 would have been worth about $1,000,000 in 1990. Franklin's calculations, barring "no unfortunate accident has prevented the operation," indicated each city would have the equivalent of $4,061,000,000 within their trust. That means, even after distributing two-thirds of the trust assets in 1890, the trust would still have grown more than 4,000 times its original value. Talk about the power of compound interest!

Perhaps the most compelling thing about Franklin's Last Will and Testament isn't just his confidence in the sanctity of self-made citizens nor his acute financial acumen, but his faith in this new experiment called "The United States of America." Remember, at the time of his passing, the U.S. Constitution was only three years old. "What's really brilliant about Ben Franklin's plan is his confidence that America would survive intact for hundreds of years," says Towarnicky.

In Franklin's mind, the 200-year trusts he established each for the cities of Boston and Philadelphia presented an experiment. In a way, he was testing the popular English proverb from a century before "A penny spar'd is twice got."[7] Rather than spend those pennies, his will saved them. Furthermore, he didn't expect them to merely double in value, but to grow exponentially as the interest accrued for two centuries.

Actually, after the first century, two-thirds of the trust was to be distributed, with the remainder left to grow. In either case, that amounts to a substantial amount of money. Maybe that's why, the September 1899 Pall Mall Magazine published the first known attribution of the adage "A penny saved is a penny earned" to Benjamin Franklin. It must have been clear by then, with the first massive distributions from the Franklin Trusts, that ol' Ben was more than mesmerized by the thought of compound interest, he was, quite simply, right about its power.

There are many methods used to show the importance of saving for retirement as early as possible. Who knew the best real-life example and the best lesson would come from one of our Founding Fathers? Ben Franklin, ever the analytical thinker, understood the power of compounding, and how time enhances that power. While others around him worried of the new country's future, Ben was busy devising a way to capitalize on that future. In doing so, he showed us by example how to use the future to our advantage. Did we learn?

CHAPTER THREE:
BEN FRANKLIN'S TRUSTS – DID THEY WORK?

The ever meticulous Benjamin Franklin sought to control at least a portion of his wealth from his grave. That particular bequest (in 1790) – 1,000 pounds sterling each to the cities of Boston and Philadelphia – came with specific directions as to its use and disbursement. These instructions covered a period of 200 years. How close did the beneficiaries stick to Franklin's instructions? How did this loyalty – or lack of loyalty – to the grantor's final wishes leave the final estate at the end of Franklin's 200-year time period? Finally, what does the legacy of Ben Franklin's Last Will and Testament tell us about ourselves, our nation, and our collective financial literacy?

Franklin calculated the value of each fund would be £131,000 at the end of the first hundred years (in 1890) of the trust. At that time, the terms of his will commanded the trustees to disperse £100,000 to the beneficiary city and continue investing the remaining £31,000 per the original guidelines. He then expected, following the next hundred years (in 1990), the total sum of each fund to be worth £4,061,000 (here he may have been a bit off since our spreadsheet "fact check" produced a sum of £4,142,455).

Chances are, if you're reading this you may be less familiar with pounds sterling compared to dollars and you most likely aren't at all aware of currency exchange rates, let alone historical currency exchange rates. Indeed, if you're like most people, you're most likely wondering "How much are each of these values worth in today's dollars?"

That's a great question. A quick trip to the internet proved no one agrees on any singular answer. There are simply too many variables over the two centuries to produce a reliable pinpoint number. The site MeasuringWorth.com, however, purports to offer "the public the highest quality and most reliable historical data on important economic aggregates, with particular emphasis on nominal (current-price) measures, as well as real (constant-price) measures. The data presented here on the United States, the United Kingdom and Australia, have been created using the highest standards of the fields of economics and history, and they were rigorously refereed by the most distinguished researchers in the fields." Because of this impressive mission and the more than a dozen members on their Board of Advisers, (all from well-regarded universities), this site seemed as good as any to get our data. Here's what we found:

The original bequest of £1,000 in 1790, the equivalent of a little bit more than $4,000 at the time according to several reports, was worth between $146,000 and $197,000 in 2014 dollars (per the MeasuringWorth.com calculator). Ben Franklin expected the trusts to be worth $637,000 apiece in 1890. Of this, $486,000 would be distributed and the remaining $151,000 would continue to be invested as originally intended. Finally, those $151,000 1890 dollars were expected to grow to $7,390,000 in 1990.

So, what happened? A lot, and apparently much of it not in keeping with Franklin's intent. "Apparently both cities originally used the funds exactly as Franklin had prescribed: a revolving loan fund for young tradesman, lending out cash at 5%," says Rose. "By the time the 100-year mark came around, however, both cities moved to generalize the "assistance to young people", and created Franklin Institutes with part of the cash (Philadelphia's became an important museum and science center, Boston's became a junior technical college with the support of Andrew Carnegie). The remaining balances were then professionally invested to generate a return, with the proceeds being used for scholarships and other worthy purposes…but not the originally intended one of supporting entrepreneurship!"

Indeed, as late as four generations after the trust was established, at least Philadelphia continued to follow Franklin's original intent. By then, the City of Philadelphia had been managing a number of charitable-minded trusts. Franklin's trust was considered a "minor" trust. In 1873, the Committee on Minor Trusts recognized there was a problem in the administration of the trust. Apparently, the maximum size of the loans may have become too small on account of inflation and general economic growth. Citing the loans "are little used, because the sum of $300, as indicated by the will, is found to be too small," the Committee "was authorized to apply to the Legislature for permission to loan to young married artificers $600 each from the Benjamin Franklin trust…"[1]

The lack of use received widespread attention outside the Philadelphia media markets. In 1878, *The Ogdensburg Advance and St. Lawrence Weekly Democrat* reported "for various reasons the young mechanics don't avail themselves of it, and the trustees are puzzling their brains to devise some means by which the intentions of the testator can be carried out and the fund kept from being idle."[2]

It may have been more than just size that mattered. Ilene Davis, author of *Wealthy by Choice: Choosing Your Way to a Wealthier Future* and a financial professional located in Cocoa, Florida, says, "Interest rates during that time likely varied (though I don't have exact numbers), and other lenders may have been willing to lend at lower rates, which borrowers would have been wise to take instead."

Within a few years, the City of Philadelphia determined it was necessary to take a different path for using the funds. It decided, since demand for small business loans was so small, to allow the trust money to be used for other types of loans. In 1885, "the superintendent of minor trusts was directed to invest $3000 from the 'Benjamin Franklin Trust' in mortgages or loans, as expressed in resolution of the board passed July 8, 1885."[3]

At the same time, it was becoming apparent the lack of use may have led to significant under-performance in the trusts, at least compared to Franklin's expectations. Citing the problem that "furnishing loans to young mechanics is an elephant on the hands of that city," officials explained, "Franklin reckoned that in 100 years the fund would amount to about $650,000 of which $500,000 should then go to the city for public improvements, and the remaining $150,000 be invested in the same way for another 100 years. The sum has amounted to be over $200,000 [between the two cities]."[4]

As the national economy developed, good borrowers were able to find better rates from other sources. Towards the end of the first hundred years, internal statistics from Boston's Franklin Trust indicated almost nine out of ten borrowers failed to repay their loan, relying instead on the co-signers to make the payment.[5] As a result, Boston stopped making loans in 1886.[6]

It gets worse. Not only did the funds trail their targets, but the values of the two cities' trusts, which theoretically should have grown by the same amount, began to diverge – and not in a small way. The Philadelphia Benjamin Franklin Trust was worth $53,500 in 1883.[7] Things did improve five years later when the annual report valued the Philadelphia Trust at $72,819, still but a fraction of what Franklin had calculated it to have become.[8] By 1890, The Boston fund must have been better managed than the Philadelphia fund, for, by Feb. 1, 1890, it had increased up to $368,741.19. It consists of $305,466.74 deposited with the Massachusetts Hospital Life Insurance company; $2,883.75 deposited in the Suffolk Savings bank; balance of bonds for loans, $390, and sixty-three cents in cash.[9] Philadelphia's Franklin Fund languished at a mere $114,000 at the 100-year mark.[10] In both cases, the totals lagged well below Franklin's expectations.

With the first century anniversary of the Franklin Trust coming, along with the first major distribution from the trusts, the worst came. "By the turn of the 20th century," says Rose, "the administration of the funds had gotten embroiled with local politics, and there were some minor scandals around one or both."

First came the inevitable suit from Franklin's descendants, who sought to prove it was inappropriate to have established the trust in the first place. On September 30, 1890, just as the first tranche was about to be distributed, *The New York Times*, with the large headline blaring "FRANKLIN'S WILL IN COURT," reported:

"PHILADELPHIA, Sept. 29.- A petition was filed in the Orphans' Court of this city today by the heirs of Benjamin Franklin, praying that the sum of $100,000 now held by the Board of City Trusts, and known as the "Franklin fund," be turned over to them, the ground for the claim being that the provisions of the will are in violation of the law, and therefore void."[11]

The Times explained to its readers "The contest is based upon several grounds, the primary and most important of which is what is known as the 'rule of perpetuities' in common law. The law does not provide for the vesting of a legacy beyond the period of twenty-one years after the lifetime of the legatee, except funds devoted to charity. It is distinctly claimed that Franklin's plan did not contemplate charity from the fact that interest was charged on the loans. The claim is also raised that the purpose of the testator has not been consummated owing to the apathy and negligence of the trustees both in this city and Boston, but more especially in this city [Philadelphia], where the principal sum has only attained about one-sixth of the proportion originally figured out."[12]

It took two years, but the heirs lost their legal battle. This news appears to have been relegated to a mere wire service story picked up by a variety of small market newspapers: "S. F. McCleary, of Brookline, Mass., treasurer of the Benjamin Franklin fund, says the supreme court of Pennsylvania has dismissed the petition of Elizabeth JD. Gillespie and Albert Duane Bache to set aside the legacies to the cities of Pennsylvania and Boston made by the will of Benjamin Franklin. The petitioners are great-grandchildren of Dr. Franklin."[13,14,15]

Then came the politics, again as evidenced in the plight of the Boston Fund. Franklin's codicil provided that the Selectmen of that city were to be among the trustees. In the century since the execution of Franklin's will, Boston had changed its governing structure from that of using Selectmen to one using a Mayor and Aldermen. It was the Aldermen, not the Mayor, that took the place of the Selectmen. When it came time to decide what to do with the scheduled hundredth year disbursement of the Trust's funds, the question of "Who rightfully constituted the trustees?" became a contentious issue. The Mayor, being an executive official like the Selectmen, felt he should represent the city as a trustee rather than the Aldermen, who were merely legislators. The Aldermen, on the other hand, were viewed as "a shifting body, and its members could not always be relied upon for intelligent, discreet action in matters of this sort." It appeared Boston might lose access to the 100-year anniversary distribution Franklin's will mandated. As part of this controversy regarding the "rightful trustee," the Corporation Counsel gave as his opinion "the trustees could not legally establish an endowment fund to carry on the school with what is left after erecting the building and equipping it with machinery, etc." It was feared the matter would soon find itself in court "to determine the exact status of the trustees, and their duties and prerogative."[16]

Eventually Boston got its school, but succeeding generations of politicians couldn't wait to get their hands on the Franklin funds. In 1930, the Massachusetts Supreme Court quashed an effort to alter control of Boston's Benjamin Franklin Trust, then valued at nearly half a million dollars.[17]

Published reports in 1951 showed the fund in Boston (at $1,043,980) had grown to be five times larger than its Philadelphia cousin ($209,031). One Boston banker bragged the difference could be explained by one simple fact: "Boston has kept the politicians out of it. They tried to get in on the fund once, but we fought them to the Massachusetts Supreme Court and won."[18]

While the Boston trustees may have successfully fought the politicians, they soon found themselves undertaking the same strategy to release the funds to those politicians. With the Boston Trust now worth $1.75 million, officials at the Franklin Foundation, the organization that was overseeing the fund, sued in court to have the Trust terminated. They complained the trust could no longer serve its purpose of providing loans to "young artificers." In March of 1960, the Massachusetts Supreme Court rejected this claim, stating local politicians would have to wait another 31 years before they could access the remnants of Franklin's will. They did, however, state that the money did not have to remain "in sterile fashion." They reinterpreted Franklin's definition of "artificer to include medical and science students, removed the marriage requirement, and reduced the interest rate from 5% to 2% (while the students were still in school, but rising again to 5% after graduation). Finally, they required the loans to be repaid within five years after graduation.[19]

At the conclusion of the Franklin Trusts' first centennial (1890), the Boston fund was about three times more than the Philadelphia fund. A half-century later, Boston was then five times larger. Oddly enough, though, when the two funds reached their termination date in 1990, Boston's trust was only twice as large as the Philadelphia trust. When the 200-year clock had run out on the Franklin Trusts, Boston had accumulated $5 million and Philadelphia's fund had grown to $2.25 million. These figures represent a far cry from Franklin's 18th century calculations, with Boston attaining roughly 66% of Franklin's goal and Philadelphia a paltry 33% of that goal.[20]

Why did Philadelphia's fund grow slower than Boston's during the 200-year span of the Trusts? Did Philadelphia really do something different to close the gap in the last 50 years of the Trusts' lives or was it something Boston did differently? The next few pages will quickly reveal what these answers tell us about the final lesson Ben Franklin may have taught us, however unintentionally.

CHAPTER FOUR:
THE TRUE LEGACY OF BEN FRANKLIN'S
LAST WILL AND TESTAMENT

Ben Franklin may have been teased into starting twin 200-year trusts in Boston and Philadelphia, but he nonetheless realized a great idea when he saw one. He even recognized the potential obstacles that might present themselves to those tasked with executing his grand plan. More important, we now recognize that, all other things aside, Franklin should be applauded for his eternal optimism in the nation he helped found.

The history of his legacy trusts – The Franklin Trust of Philadelphia and the Franklin Foundation of Boston – instructs us on both the power of compound interest and the dangers of relying on public officials to manage money for the long-term. We might even call it "The Tale of Two Trusts."

In Franklin's calculations, the value of both the Boston and Philadelphia Trusts should have been identical after 200 years. Why did Philadelphia's fund grow slower than Boston's? Ilene Davis says, "If they had been invested for the same time at the same rate, there would be no difference, so it would appear that Philly got lower returns on funds invested than Boston."

Rose believes the "differences in the remaining funds after 200 years, have very little to do with the way the funds were invested, and much more to do with politics and the uses to which the funds were put. But the essential takeaway here is that Franklin established the funds as a debt fund, with a prescribed 5% return, which meant that, assuming full utilization, he could project exactly what the balances would be in 100 and 200 years. Had Franklin instead taken a 21st century approach and made them equity funds, investing for partial ownership in the businesses being created (for various reasons that wasn't practical back then), then one of two things would have happened: either the funds would have evaporated early in the 19th century when the large majority of the businesses failed… or it would today be the world's largest charitable fund, likely worth many tens of billions of dollars. Such is the leverage of equity!"

What likely caused the trusts to miss their modest targets (remember, Franklin assumed only a mere 5% annual growth rate) could be attributed, at least in part, to the changing economic landscape. This applies both to the nature of business and interest rates. The industrial revolution wiped out the need for small entrepreneurs (or "artisans" as Franklin called them). At the same time, overall economic growth reduced the cost of capital, bringing lending rates down for all but the riskiest borrowers.

These factors, however, were recognized and addressed within the first hundred years of the trust. Despite these impediments, Boston came within 57% of attaining Franklin's 1890 goal. Philadelphia, however, missed the mark considerably, managing a very weak 18% of Franklin's estimate.

From the beginning, it was clear the two funds would be managed in different styles, given the different corporate structures of the host cities. Control of the Boston funds remained in private hands for the longest time. Philadelphia very quickly placed responsibility for the Franklin Trust in the hands of a political committee. Alas, as time marched on, the politicians marched in, and Boston's Franklin fund could not escape this inevitability.

While Philadelphia had this struggle in the latter half of the nineteenth century, Boston went through this phase in earnest during the post-World War II era. This had a dramatic impact on the outcome of the trust's growth. By the early 1950s, the Boston Trust was valued at five times more than the Philadelphia Trust and well on its way of making up ground lost at the 1890 accounting. At the time of the trust termination date, though, the Boston fund was only twice that of the Philadelphia fund. In the end, the Boston fund missed Franklin's target by nearly 33%. Philadelphia missed it by almost 70%.

Still, it does show something that an initial investment of about $9,000 in 1790 could grow to a total value of $7.25 million some two hundred years later. That's certainly a testament to the power of compound interest – the very thing Franklin counted on and wanted to demonstrate.

Indeed, this obvious success inspired at least one copy-cat trust. On November 12, 1928, Jacob Friedrich Schoellkopf, Jr., an industrialist from Buffalo, New York, established the Jacob F.-Wilma S. Schoellkopf $100,000 Trust Fund for Buffalo. This fund was set up like the Franklin Trust save for one very important difference: It had no termination date. It would accumulate and reinvest all income for the first 100 years, upon which 50% of its value would be distributed. From then on, the remaining undistributed portion would be reinvested and, every fifty years in perpetuity, half the value of the fund would be distributed.[1]

Also unlike the Franklin trusts, there appears to have been no major restrictions on the type of investments in which the Schoellkopf Fund could be placed. In addition – and here is a key distinguishing difference – the Schoellkopf Fund was completely private. It involved no elected officials. Even the distributions went to a private foundation, not one run by political authorities.

Could this have given the Schoellkopf Fund an advantage in terms of its growth prospects. In the 1950s, Boston's Franklin Trust grew 75%. The Schoellkopf Fund grew 285% during the same period.[2]

It may not have been the intention of the ever-optimistic Ben Franklin, but the faithful execution of the codicil in his last will and testament proved, over its 200-year lifespan, that there may be a greater harm to long-term growth prospects than either war or economic calamities. The Franklin trusts, administered by public officials, may have demonstrated more than the success of compound interest. They may have inadvertently revealed the potential for significant damage when we place elected officials in the position to oversee long-term monies.

Towarnicky explains the shortfall of the Franklin Trusts in blunt terms. He says, "It isn't clear, but I believe the worst shortcoming comes from giving governments control." Perhaps Jack bases that conclusion on what we've seen over the last 80 years when it comes to government managed long-term investments. It didn't always use to be that way. For most of our nation's history, and especially during the first century-and-a-half of its existence, Americans have had a very different view of retirement than they have today.

How can this traditional perspective on retirement – born before the dawn of the Industrial Age – enlighten us given today's very different understanding? It turns out, after looking at the contemporary record, we can find answers to today's most pressing questions. Join me as we discover these answers together in the next few chapters.

SECTION TWO:

– FROM THE LENS OF HISTORY –

AMERICA, AMERICANS, AND THE CULTURE OF RETIREMENT

CHAPTER FIVE:
RIPPED FROM TODAY'S HEADLINES:
THE LOOMING RETIREMENT CRISIS

Warning: The following few chapters contain alarming media screeches, arcane facts, and numerical figures intended for curious audiences and is not suitable for people with no interest in current events, bored by American history, and deathly afraid of math. Reader discretion is advised.

Helaine Olen summed up the key point of her March 4, 2016 *Slate* article "The Retirement Crisis Is Getting Truly Scary" with this stark reality:

"And so once again, it seems we're in a mess of trouble—and we know it. A recent survey by employer consultant Willis Towers Watson of almost 5,100 employed Americans found that 76 percent of them said they believed they would fare 'much worse' in retirement than their moms and dads. Not just worse, mind you. Much worse. Almost one-third think they will run out of money within 15 years of leaving the workforce."[1]

This isn't a problem limited to pundits, either. Regular salt-of-the-earth people see this foreboding omen, too. Experts hear stories from the front lines of the retirement crisis every day. Peter Dunn writes regularly for *USA TODAY* under the name "Pete the Planner." In his July 22, 2017 column titled "Tackling Baby Boomers' retirement crisis," a millennial couple asked a financial question about their retired baby boomer parents. Dunn led off his response with "Your question… illuminates the retirement crises facing so many of the estimated 10,000 Baby Boomers who retire every day…"[2]

There's a growing sense that Baby Boomers, long used to getting things their way, (remember, they were called the "Me Generation" in the 1960s), are about to find out the hard way the truth behind the Rolling Stones classic rock-and-roll anthem "You Can't Always Get What You Want." According to research published by GoBankingRates, 30% of the people over the age of 55 responded they did not have anything saved for retirement, while another 26% said they had saved less than $50,000 for retirement.[3] It doesn't take Mick Jagger to tell you those folks likely can't get no satisfaction in their retirement years.

The news only gets worse. A survey conducted by the Insured Retirement Institute revealed that a mere 23% of Americans aged 54 to 70 thought they had enough savings to carry them through retirement.[4] This only makes sense since, in the same survey, we see 60% didn't even bother to try to figure out how much money they needed in retirement.[5] It's data like this that makes a compelling case that America is heading for a retirement crisis.

The retirement crisis, however, is not limited to only Baby Boomers. Wendy Connick, in her June 17, 2017 article for *The Motley Fool* titled "Are We Facing a Retirement Crisis?" says "Every generation faces challenges when it comes to funding retirement, but this time, a number of different challenges are all coming together at once." Calling it "A retirement perfect storm," she cites four reasons for the looming crisis: 1) The demographic bulge known as the Baby Boomers is squeezing the money out of Social Security and Medicare; 2) All generations aren't saving enough to meet their projected retirement needs; 3) The 2008/2009 market crash set back what little savings everyone had; and, 4) Still shell-shocked by the memory of the free fall in stock prices, retirement savers, who require long-term growth investments, have been reluctant to return to equities, the most reliable long-term growth investment.[6]

Connick's last item sums up the entire philosophy of behavioral economics, which is, and I paraphrase, "people are stupid." You might think this sounds mean, but it's a lot more charitable than the more appropriate response, which is, "people are crazy." OK, that time it did sound mean. What I mean to say is "people aren't rational." And if you still think that's a nasty thing to say, then I must remind you where that phrase comes from.

But first, a WARNING. The following gets into the thicket of the academic. If you don't like such thickets, skip the next three paragraphs. If you enjoy hacking your way through this sort of underbrush, then proceed under your own risk. If you enjoy skewering all things academic, then, as you read the next three paragraphs, try to keep your snickering down so as to not disturb those around you.

There's a financial theory called "Modern Portfolio Theory." The theory's basis is an imaginative construct commonly known as "the Efficient Market Hypothesis." It's called a "hypothesis" because researchers aren't really sure that it's right. So unsure are these academics that they've come up with three different flavors for this hypothesis (they call them "variations," but most people know more about ice cream than high finance, so I'm sticking with "flavors"). The flavors are "Strong," "Semi-Strong," and "Weak."

What's the difference between the flavors? Literally, the "rationality" of the buyers and sellers in the market. Let me translate this in terms of *Star Trek*. Mr. Spock represents the "Strong" version, Captain Kirk stands for the "Semi-Strong" option; and poor Dr. McCoy is the "Weak" alternative. You know what I mean here. Mr. Spock is the logical or totally "rational" left side of the brain; Dr. McCoy is the emotional or "less-than-rational" right side of the brain; and Captain Kirk smiles as some happy medium between the two extremes.

But, wait! I said "irrational" and, certainly, Dr. McCoy may be emotional, but he's hardly irrational (well, except for maybe that time when he accidentally injected the hypo of cordrazine into his bloodstream during the teaser scene of "The City on the Edge of Forever," perhaps the greatest *Star Trek* episode). What does this tell you about the Efficient Market Hypothesis? Those smart quants that came up with it left out a flavor. (To be fair, they had to, because this particular flavor invalidates their hypothesis.) Namely, what if the market is not merely "weak" when it comes to rationality, what if it is downright irrational? In keeping with the genre, let's say this fourth flavor is represented by the character Jar Jar Binks. "What?" you might ask? Here's the answer: Jar Jar Binks signifies the irrational option – the option that wholly rejects the Efficient Market Hypothesis. The choice of the *Star Wars* character Jar Jar Binks doesn't simply play on the looneyness of Jar Jar, but also the fact that it's crazy to even place a *Star Wars* character within the same universe of a *Star Trek* metaphor!

Welcome back all those who skipped the last three paragraphs, although, I must admit, if you're a sci-fi fan, you might want to go back and read them. Those that did read them might be wondering, "Why the intergalactic interlude? We're talking about the retirement crisis, aren't we?" Well, yes, and we're specifically referring to Connick's last item: the fear of returning to the market. (Here's a clue for you all: "Fear" is an emotion and emotions are, by definition, irrational.) This is what Ben Carlson, Director of Institutional Asset Management at Ritholtz Wealth Management and author of the books *A Wealth of Common Sense: Why Simplicity Trumps Complexity in Any Investment Plan* and *Organizational Alpha: How to Add Value in Institutional Asset Management*, has to say on the significance of Connick's fourth reason we sit on the precipice of a retirement crisis:

> *"There are many baby boomers who squandered the opportunity for large gains in financial assets because they didn't have any money at stake. I'm sure most of those who are underprepared right now for retirement would tell you they wish they would have saved more money when they were younger. You could have the best investment strategy on the planet but it won't help you if you don't save money to take advantage. The best investment you can make is often saving more money."[7]*

Carlson didn't get back to me prior to the publication deadline of *From Cradle to Retirement*, so I don't know if the planet he refers to is part of the *Star Trek* or *Star Wars* lexicon. (Perhaps he read my email and thought I was having a Jar Jar moment.)

How do we get here from there? Why didn't earlier generations of Americans face this same retirement dilemma? Shouldn't nearly 225 years of government oversight have finally solved the problem of lack of preparedness for the post-employment age of our oldest citizens? A quick look at our country's collective cultural attitude regarding retirement reveals an obvious answer that might genuinely surprise you.

CHAPTER SIX:
AMERICAN ATTITUDES ON RETIREMENT FROM THE REVOLUTION THROUGH WORLD WAR I

B en Franklin wrote in his famous autobiography "Lose no time; be always employ'd in something useful; cut off all unnecessary actions." He paraphrased his thoughts on idleness of all forms, not just retirement, when in the same volume he added "...there will be sleeping enough in the grave...." That, in a nutshell, sums up quite neatly the general consensus of Americans regarding the concept of retirement for the first hundred and fifty years of our country's existence. "Don't stop working" and "Work 'til you drop."

Today we might say Franklin had the luxury of living in an era of short life expectancies. He and his Revolutionary War era peers needn't worry about retirement because, chances are, they'd die before they got there. Indeed, looking at the average life expectancy of about 35[1] does lead one to this conclusion. Of course, as Franklin's sardonic heir Mark Twain said, "There are lies, damn lies, and statistics." Since early deaths can skew the life expectancy at birth (about half of those born in the 1700s died before age 20[2]), it's often better to look at life expectancies at more advance ages. For example, just because 2% of the population in 1775 was over the age of 65[3], doesn't mean people didn't live well beyond that (Franklin lived until age 84 and the first ten presidents died at an average age of 77.4 years[4]).

Yet, we rarely hear of our Founding Fathers bragging about their pensions or their summer homes in Florida. Evidently, they agree with Ben Franklin's virtue of Industry and kept their noses to whatever stones they had that needed grinding. It wasn't that they were all farmers, either. While agriculture was among the top producing occupations (particularly in the South), equally lucrative professions included those acting as merchants, lawyers, and tavern keepers (the latter often pulling in the equivalent of $100,000 a year).[5] It wasn't just farmers that found something to keep them busy in their old age, it was something all citizens of the former Colonies expected of themselves.

There was one exception, though, that proved the rule. Revolutionary War veterans who suffered injuries during the War often couldn't find meaningful employment. As a means to compensate these heroes, the young government tried to create a federally funded and administered pension plan for these veterans. This effort, while not novel (the Roman Emperor Augustus paid his legionnaires a pension[6]), showed that America's initial efforts proved controversial.

On the heels of earlier less-than-successful attempts by the Continental Congress and individual states, a 1792 Congressional Act to create a "pension list of such disabled officers and soldiers" took several tries before passing muster with the Supreme Court.[7] The idea behind this pension was honorable – Patriots who lost their ability to work in service to their country ought to be appreciated and helped financially. The Act inspired other state and municipal governments to adopt similar pension policies for their civilian workers. For example, the City of New York established a fund for "relief of disabled and indigent Firemen, and their families…" in 1791 and, in fact, paid out £126 in "pensions to sundry widows" from December 7, 1802 to December 6, 1803."[8]

The federal Revolutionary War veteran pension proved difficult to administer and quite narrow in scope. For example, a portion of the report from the House of Representatives on December 30, 1801 reads as follows:

> *"A report was presented from the same [ways and means] committee on the petition of Edward Armstrong who solicited a pension on account of wounds received in the revolutionary war. The claim was barred by the statute of limitation, therefore they though it ought not to be granted. The house agreed to the report."*[9]

Congress spent several years trying to decide what to do. President James Monroe signed the definitive pension law in 1818.[10] At that time the law was broadened to accept more veterans. In the ensuing decades, it continued to be liberalized until the pension covered the lifespans of all widows and orphans. Note the last major change in the law occurred in 1878, when all widows were included (not just widows who married the veteran during or before the Revolutionary War.)[11]

The timing of this last act, in particular, could not have been worse for public perception regarding federal administration of retirement pensions. In 1878, Commissioners of Pensions John A. Bentley said, "I am convinced that a great number of persons have been pensioned who have no just title, and that the number of that class is being constantly increased in the settlements which are now going on."[12]

This comment referred not to the Revolutionary War veterans' pensions, but the newly enacted Civil War veterans' pension. On July 14, 1862, Congress passed the first of many acts designed to provide pensions to those veterans of the Union cause (the Southern states would provide a similar pension to the Confederate veterans) which became the foundation for our modern Social Security System.[13] Enacted during an era of growing mistrust over government corruption, and the lingering distrust of centralized federal government that began with our nation's founding, the popular view of these government pensions was, well, unpopular. In the January 1893 issue of *Harper's*, we see the following written in regard to (primarily Civil War veteran) pension fraud, "In numerous communities throughout the land respectable citizens believe that they have among them some flagrant instance of dishonest pension... There is a growing conviction that the government is being shamefully plundered through the pension system; and the existence of this belief, whatever the fact, with acquiescence in the supposed abuse, cannot but have a most demoralizing influence on the public conscience... The suspicion is abroad that a mercenary spirit, incompatible with that lofty sense of honor which the popular imagination would fain attribute to its military heroes, is spreading among them. This suspicion may be unjust, but its increasing prevalence is no less sure than it is unfortunate."[14]

Modern research substantiates these fraud claims, although it can't determine the exact amount of fraud that occurred. In 1992, Theda Skocpol, Victor S. Thomas Professor of Government and Sociology at Harvard University, concluded:

> *"After poring over Annual Reports of Commissioners of Pensions to find any possible systematic statistics, I have reluctantly concluded that nothing exact can be said about the proportions of illegitimate pensioners or expenditures. We can only speculate that some (undetermined) thousands, or conceivably tens of thousands, of the nearly one million pensioners in 1910 were bogus. Perhaps aided by dishonest pension attorneys, these men and women had exploited the loose and locally rooted application system to obtain fraudulent pensions or – in most cases, I suspect – overly generous benefits."[15]*

Within this context, then, we have the 1878 law which allows all Revolutionary War widows to receive their late husband's Revolutionary War veteran's pension. Consider the math for a moment. This law was passed more than one hundred years after the start of the Revolutionary War, meaning any surviving veteran would have been at least 108 years old at the time! Let's put this in some perspective. Lemuel Cook is considered the last "official" Revolutionary War veteran to die. He died on May 20, 1866 at the age of 106. Of course, Cook is merely the last truly documented veteran (he was discharged by none other than George Washington). There's a claim on the part of one Daniel Bakeman, who died at age 109 on April 5, 1869. Although he never had proper papers, Congress nonetheless awarded him pension for service during the Revolutionary War.[16]

In either case, all Revolutionary War veterans were dead by the time of the 1878 act to give their pension to their widows. What was up with that?

The last surviving widow of a Revolutionary War soldier was Mrs. Esther Sumer Damon. She died on November 11, 1906, 131 years after "the shot heard 'round the world."[17] She was 93 years old when she died, the same age that her husband Noah Damon was when he died. Of course, he was 54 years older than Esther (he died in 1853). Both their marriage (in 1835 when she was 21 and he was 75) and his death predated the 1878 act that allowed widows to collect the Revolutionary War veteran's pension for remainder of their life. It seems unlikely their marriage was a sham. As a matter of fact, Noah didn't even claim his pension until 1848 13 years after he married Esther.[18]

The same can't be said for the Civil War veterans. It seems the feds were on the case for last minute May-December marriages. The strategy was quite simple. The young bride would marry the aging veteran, then would immediate desert her husband, only to reappear following the veteran's death to lay claim on the widow's pension. These marriages would most often occur near government maintained old soldiers' homes. Of these, the Soldiers' Home in Hampton, Virginia had the dishonor of hosting the most of these fraudulent marriages.[19]

To remedy this apparently all-too-common practice, Congress enacted legislation on March 3, 1899 prohibiting widows from collecting pensions unless their marriage to the veteran "was duly and legally contracted and entertained into prior to the passage of this act, or unless such wife shall have lived and cohabited with such soldier continuously from the date of the marriage to the date of his death or unless the marriage shall take place hereafter and prior to or during the military or naval service of the soldier." [20]

Yet, Civil War pensions were paid out to widows into the twenty-first century. That's right. That means pension payments covered three centuries. The last Civil War widow, Maudie Cecilia Hopkins, died on August 17, 2008 at the Helena Medical Center in Helena, Arkansas at the age of – you guessed it – 93. She had married Confederate veteran William Cantrell in August of 1932. At the time, he was 86 and she was 19. He died three years later, but she never claimed his widow's pension.[21]

The distinction of last surviving pension widow goes to another Confederate widow, Alberta Martin, who died on May 31, 2004 at a nursing home in Alabama. She was 97 years old. At the age of 21, she married 81-year-old William Martin on December 10, 1927. Given the age of William, it's amazing then that, ten months after their marriage, the couple produced a son. After 4 years of marriage, William passed away and Alberta lived for many years in obscure poverty.[22] Her story was discovered decades later and in September 1996 she finally began receiving the Civil War widow's pension she was eligible for.[23]

Incidentally, the last Union widow to collect a Civil War pension died only a few months before her Confederate counterpart. Gertrude Janeway passed away on January 17, 2003. She was, um, dare I say, 93 years old. She had married John Janeway in 1927. He was 81 and she was 18.[24]

Gertrude was more than a trivial footnote, though. The story of her long-term pension payout became the lead paragraph in a major international expose on the dangers of defined benefit plans. How did these veteran pensions signal the problems and ultimate demise of corporate pension plans? Discover the answer in our next chapter.

CHAPTER SEVEN:
THE RISE AND DEMISE OF
THE CORPORATE PENSION

I n April of 2001, *The Economist* decided to write a story exposing the unfortunate mathematical vulnerability of pensions. The well-respected international financial periodical chose to lead off with this sentence: "When Gertrude Janeway died in 2003, she was still getting a monthly cheque for $70 from the Veterans Administration— for a military pension earned by her late husband, John, on the Union side of the American civil war that ended in 1865."[1] The very next paragraph summarized the article's stern warning:

> *"A pension promise can be easy to make but expensive to keep. The employers who promised higher pensions in the past knew they would not be in their posts when the bill became due. That made it tempting for them to offer higher pensions rather than better pay. Over the past 15 years the economics of the deal have become clear, initially in the private sector, where pensions (and health-care costs after retirement) were central to the bankruptcy of General Motors and many other firms."*[2]

In days of old, they roamed the annals of the corporate benefits arena like the proverbial big man strutting on campus. They represented the Holy Grail of corporate America during the era of the Organizational Man (that would be the 1950s for those too young to remember). But, like so many great inventions before them, they calcified into something akin to a boulder-like albatross dangling from a noose around their sponsoring companies' necks. Today, while a few fossils remain, they represent the exception rather than the rule. They've become a mere footnote from a time before workers gained their independence. They now represent an era of the distant past, when paternalism reigned, shackling individuals to lock-step conformity.

What led to the fall of the American Pension? Once a sign of enlightened progress, it has grown to symbolize economic stagnation and defeat. Much has been written lamenting the near extinction of the corporate pension plan. Are reports shaded by rose-colored glasses? Pension and retirement experts familiar with the history of defined benefit plans have a rather different view.

The shift from an agrarian economy to a manufacturing economy prompted the need for some basic form of pension. In 1875, the American Express Company become the first private company in the United States to offer a pension plan.[3] Robb Hill, President of R Hill Enterprises, Inc. in Aurora, Illinois, says the benefit came about "because of the industrial revolution. Manufacturing needed a lot of workers. Where were they going to get these workers from? The answer: from all the farmers and the small business owners of that time. The owners of industry realized that in order to get these people to leave their farms and their small businesses, there had to be an incentive. This is where the promise of '30 years working here and the company will take care of you in your old age' came about."

After ERISA, but before the introduction of the 401k plan, the downward trend of pensions continued through the 1980s. Again, this was before the 401k plan really took off. Only 38% of workers were covered by pension plans in 1980, while a mere seven years later that number had fallen further to just 31%. Ted Benna, the "father" of the 401k, says, "There is a widely held perception that we once had a wonderful retirement system where all employees received a pension. Only roughly 30% of the private work force were covered by pension plans when 401k hit the market. You couldn't participate in the plan Provident Mutual had when I worked until age 30 if you were a male and 35 if you were a female. You had to stay until age 60 to have any vested benefits!!! In addition, when companies failed prior to ERISA, a large portion of the pension benefits were lost when an underfunded plan was terminated. It was far from a wonderful system."

"ERISA?" You say you're not familiar with ERISA? "ERISA" stands for the "Employee Retirement Income Security Act." President Gerald Ford signed the ERISA legislation on Labor Day in 1974. ERISA came about as a result of several high-profile pension failures, as well as a very effective media campaign. "The major events that stimulated the passage of ERISA were the Studebaker plan termination in the early 1960s, subsequent hearings that were held about pensions in response, the 1972 NBC documentary 'Pensions: The Broken Promise' (see http://archives.nbclearn.com/portal/site/k-12/flatview?cuecard=57200), and the Ralph Nader book *You and Your Pension*, published in 1973," says Mitchell Langbert, Associate Professor Brooklyn College Koppelman School of Business. "Some of the problems included abuse of break in service rules, underfunding or pay-as-you-go funding, and unfair benefit accrual and vesting arrangements. Nader talks about them in his book."

From the start, ERISA gave all the appearance of being very successful. "ERISA was intended to protect employee rights. ERISA's eligibility, vesting, and funding requirements accomplished that very well," says Bruce Gendein, president of The Senex Group and a specialist in tax-qualified retirement plans in Woodland Hills, California.

The termination of the Studebaker pension plan highlighted the problems addressed by ERISA. "There were essentially no funding requirements prior to ERISA, so a company could promise all these benefits in their defined benefits plan, but there was no obligation to set money aside to fund those promises," says Adam Pozek, a partner and retirement plan consultant at DWC: The 401k Experts, based in St. Paul, Minnesota. "The other issue was that any money that was set aside wasn't protected and was accessible by creditors to satisfy legal judgments, or by employers that wanted to use the money for other purposes (honorable or nefarious). ERISA was quite effective at addressing both these issues. It put protections in that require employers to fund defined benefit plans on an ongoing basis and it posed restrictions so that once the money was set aside, it couldn't come back out for the employer's use without being hit with a substantial excise tax. It also protects plan assets from creditors and legal judgments. As with any complicated law, in retrospect, you always see things that could have been done differently. Based on the objectives it was trying to achieve, it did an admirable job."

But from these seeds of glory rose the monster that many believe would ultimately do in the pension plan. "ERISA was created, in part, to provide greater security to participants and beneficiaries," says Robin M. Solomon, an attorney in the Employee Benefits and Executive Compensation practice of Ivins, Phillips & Barker in Washington, D.C. "It met this goal in several respects. It created a system of federal insurance through the Pension Benefit Guaranty Corporation ("PBGC") to guarantee the payment of benefits whenever a covered plan terminates with insufficient assets. It also established access to federal courts, where participants could recover benefits or enforce their rights to recover damages on behalf of the plan."

ERISA created the PBGC to prevent the Studebaker fiasco from happening again. While a noble, and in some ways successful, intention, the law of unintended consequences soon reared its ugly head. "I used to sell defined benefit pension plans prior to the passage of ERISA," says Benna. "It became impossible to sell them post ERISA due to the way PBGC is structured. The maximum benefit limits that were also part of ERISA played a major role in breaking the financial linkage of senior executives from rank and file employees. This was followed by the adoption of new accounting rules that made quarterly pension expenses very unpredictable. This financial uncertainty pressured senior executives to dump pension plans in an attempt to help drive up earnings thereby increasing the stock value for the benefit of shareholders and themselves. The defined benefit system would be dying even if 401k never happened and it will continue to die even if 401k is shut down tomorrow. I don't rejoice that the defined benefit system is dying but it is a reality."

In December of 1985, the Financial Accounting Standards Board released "Statement No. 87" (commonly referred to as "FASB 87"). FASB 87 changed the accounting reporting requirements for pensions, and this had a dramatic impact on all corporations offering pensions, most acutely among publicly traded companies. "FASB 87 required the use of the unit credit actuarial cost method in the context of recognition of pension liabilities on corporate balance sheets," says Langbert. "At that time managers were increasingly concerned about bottom-line performance because of an increasing emphasis on stock options in executive compensation. Anything that could boost stock performance in the short term meant potential returns to stock options, which magnify stock price volatility. Increased liabilities from pensions meant that a hostile takeover that involved a plan termination might boost balance sheet equity, hence the stock value."

In requiring full accrual-based disclosure of pension liabilities and assets, FASB inadvertently provided vital information to arbitrage specialists. Indeed, this was precisely the theme posed in the 1987 hit movie *Wall Street*. In that film, where Michael Douglass' character Gordon Gekko famously declares "Greed is good," we see the harsh reality of mathematics. Under the tutelage of Gekko, Charlie Sheen's Bud Fox discovers the company his father (both literally and in the story, as the character was played by Martin Sheen) works for is worth more in liquidation than as a continuing operating business. Fox must decide whether to side with the dispassionate truth of corporate Darwinism or succumb to the emotion of family ties.

This Hollywood story was really "ripped from the headlines," as such corporate takeovers were occurring regularly in the 1980s. "In many cases, like TWA, the corporate raiders used the companies' overfunded pension plans to finance the takeover by terminating the pension plan, reverting the excess assets back to the company to be used as part of the takeover financing," says Gendein. "It became a problem to the extent that Congress instituted a 50% excise penalty to discourage the practice. Pension plans move from overfunded to underfunded and back as funding and economic conditions change."

As Benna states, the decline in pension plans began as soon as President Ford signed ERISA into law. "There was a gradual trend after passage of ERISA" says Langbert. "The compliance costs of regulation likely encouraged the trend toward plan termination. As well, global competitive pressures in the manufacturing sector made firms more cost-and-risk conscious. I recall the regulatory environment in the 1980s (ironically, during the Reagan years) as one of almost the end of the rule of law. Regulations were being passed so quickly and extensively that I was getting jet lag attending ERISA Industry Committee meetings. Large firms don't mind constant regulatory shifts. However, I know of smaller firms that have been destroyed by regulation like MEPPAA (the MEPPAA stands for Multi-Employer Pension Plan Amendment Act)."

Pozek saw the first decline start between 1985 and 1990, followed by an even bigger drop-off from 1990-1995. "Since then," he says, "the number of plans has remained relatively constant. There are a number of factors that have prompted private businesses to move away from defined benefit plans, but the primary reason is cost. As workforces and plan sizes have grown, these plans have become more expensive to maintain. Volatility in the stock market makes it harder to predict potential cash flow hits, and a drop in the market can lead to unexpected and significant expenses."

The demise of the corporate pension plan in America, however, cannot be limited to domestic policy and actions alone. "Large public companies moved away from defined benefit plans when they started to compete internationally with companies in other countries who did not provide the same wage and benefit levels," says Gendein.

To read the headlines today gives the appearance there's a consensus among retirement policy pundits that "things would be better if only we had our old pensions back." Despite these rosy memories, actual history shows, with a few notable exceptions, pensions were never as universal or as lucrative as imagined. Nor have corporate expenditures receded as much as it seems. "There's a lot of talk in the media about how employers aren't spending as much on benefits," says Pozek, "but if you look back to the mid-80s, the bureau of labor statistics shows that the typical increase in wages has been in the neighborhood of 140%, and there has been an increase of spending on retirement benefits of about 150%. But over that time period, employers have had to increase their spending on health benefits by almost 255%. So, you can't look at the death of one benefit just on its own, you have to look at what else employers are spending on. The money has to come from somewhere. It's a combination of all these factors that have put pressure on each other. There has to be a give and take on what employers are spending on."

The larger truth we must face, though, deals not with dollars, but with change (and not the small kind). The world that birthed pensions no longer exists. The change from the industrial age changed the working habits of families and created a need for a "corporate" retirement. Is it surprising, then, as we evolve from a population dominated by factory and office workers to one dominated by workers engaged in ever changing gigs, that our definition of retirement will also change? And with that change in definition comes a change in the logistics of the preparation for and delivery of that retirement. "Pensions depend on a corporate feudalism that the labor economist Arthur Ross noticed in the 1950s," says Langbert. "The labor market became more flexible because of global pressures, so the 20-year vesting schedules that existed before ERISA failed to address the needs of Boomers entering the labor market in the 1970s. The picture of stable employment relationships received a death blow when IBM had mass layoffs in the early 1990s."

In theory, the traditional corporate pension plan remains as originally advertised. Unfortunately, in practice, today's work environment just can't meet the assumptions of that theory. Pozek says, "I don't think that the corporate pension plan necessarily failed to provide an adequate retirement income. The workers who were covered by plans did receive pretty good benefits. However, as the plans became more expensive to maintain, you had fewer and fewer employers offering them and, therefore, fewer and fewer employees who were covered by them. The other factor that might lead to the impression that these plans fail to provide adequate retirement income is that they were designed at a time when someone landed a job and stayed there their entire career. These plans rewarded longevity, so they would pay out bigger benefits the longer an employee stayed. The average job tenure started to drop off from the mid to late 80s to today. Now, in certain segments of the workforce, the average tenure is less than 3 years. That's a far cry from getting to a company and staying there for 30 years. So, with shorter job tenure, you have a shorter amount of time to accrue benefits."

We tend to forget that the greatest value of a pension occurs in the final years of employment. With the trend in job-hopping, it's less likely workers will ever get to those "final" years. "The actuarial value of a pension benefit builds dramatically from ages 50 to 65," says Benna. "Having a pension is great if you stay with one employer for 30 plus years, and are covered by a final average pay plan. They don't work well if you change jobs multiple times. In fact, an employee builds very little value prior to age 35 in a standard pension plan. As a result, agonizing over reviving defined benefit plans make sense only if we expect future employees to have only one or two employers during their careers that are willing to assume the financial risks related to such plans."

So, why are pension expenditures increasing in the face of fewer and fewer eligible pensioners retiring from the workforce? Again, we must concede to that awful curmudgeon, math. Oh, and increasing life expectancy. "Contrary to long-held beliefs, corporate retirement pension plans were never intended to provide adequate income for retirees, says Gendein. "These plans were only intended to provide for part of an employee's retirement income as one leg of the proverbial 3-legged stool, with the other two 'legs' being social security and personal savings. Even so, as workers' life spans grew over the past few decades, there was an important paradigm shift: rather than providing a pension for 5, 10, or 15 years, suddenly these plans were expected to pay an employee for 2 or 3 decades of retirement. That means that if an employee had worked for the company for 30 years and lived in retirement for 20, the company was in effect paying them for 50 years. It created a very difficult – if not impossible – scenario in a competitive world."

In 2005, two years after the last surviving Civil War widow died, thus ending Civil War veteran pension payouts, Roger Lowenstein wrote in *The New York Times Magazine*, "It is not hedge funds or the real-estate bubble – it is the pension system, both public and private. And it is broken."[4]

There's no point trying to put the proverbial genie of the pension plan back in its nineteenth century bottle. Our country, our culture, and our economy has moved on. Lowenstein may not have been referring to it specifically, but the next chapter explores the reality of his sentiments as applied to the ultimate public pension.

CHAPTER EIGHT:
A PROMISE BREAKING

Franklin D. Roosevelt, in justifying his effort to pass the Social Security Act of 1935, offered this promise: "The Social Security Act was primarily designed to provide the average worker with same assurance that when cycles of unemployment come or when his working days are over, he will have enough money to live decently... It is the foundation upon which we hope in America to provide a real form of financial security for workers, so that the spectre of unemployment and old-age destitution may be banished from the American home and farm."[1] Does this promise continue to be fulfilled, or, as many believe, has it been slowly breaking over the decades since its inception? Let's look at how the most recent Trustees Report addresses this matter.

When the 2017 Old-Age, Survivors, and Disability Insurance (OASDI) trustees submitted their annual report to Congress on July 13, 2017, it contained some good news and some bad news. In the good news, the report, formally referred to as "<u>The 2017 Annual Report of the Board of Trustees of the Federal Old-Age and Survivors Insurance and Federal Disability Insurance Trust Funds</u>," suggested the financial situation of the Social Security Trust Fund had improved from the previous year. On the other hand, it bluntly states "reserves become depleted in 2034." Oh, that wasn't the bad news. This is: The report goes on further to say "If substantial actions are deferred for several years, the changes necessary to maintain Social Security solvency would be concentrated on fewer years and fewer generations. Much larger changes would be necessary if action is deferred until the combined trust fund reserves become depleted in 2034."

Yes, this sounds dire, and people have a right to be alarmed, and they are. A 2015 Bankrate.com survey revealed "3 in 10 people under age 50 believe Social Security will have run dry by the time they file for benefits."[2]

This may be an overreaction. Timothy G. Wiedman, retired Associate Professor of Management & Human Resources at Doane University in Crete, Nebraska, says, "While the Social Security System will empty its so-called "trust fund" by the end of 2034 and begin running a deficit if Congress fails to make any changes, the current 12.4% payroll tax will still continue to generate billions upon billions of dollars for the system to disburse in the form of benefits." Indeed, the OASDI Report states "After trust fund reserve depletion, continuing income is sufficient to support expenditures at a level of 77 percent of program cost for the rest of 2034, declining to 73 percent for 2091."

Technical details like this, though, don't erase the fact that the promise of Social Security has long been broken – and continues to be breaking as we move further from FDR's original pronouncement. "The fact is, Social Security promises have been broken for years" says Ilene Davis. "It was supposed to max out at 1% each of income up to $3,000. It was never supposed to be taxable. Now anyone with a decent pension and some retirement funds is likely having to include 85% of their Social Security benefit as income – at a 25% tax bracket (not high) that's effectively greater than a 20% ACTUAL REDUCTION in retirement benefits when you subtract the applicable taxes from the benefits. And, of course, the Medicare premium increases – but only for those who were responsible enough to build wealth. Moreover, Social Security doesn't provide benefits, as originally promised, based on contributions. It rewards lower income workers at expense of higher income workers. All in all, a system totally biased in favor of the 'less fortunate'. It's nothing but another program to take money from those who took responsibility for their future to those who didn't."

Although considered sacrosanct today, Social Security was controversial from the moment of its inception and through its first several decades. It survived an initial constitutional challenge. In 1937, the Supreme Court ruled in favor of the act in the cases of Helvering vs. Davis, and Steward Machine Co. vs. Davis.[3] Even before the onset of hostilities of the second World War, Social Security's exposed underbelly of fiscal vulnerability became apparent. In February of 1940, former Congressman turned journalist Samuel B. Pettengill wrote this in his column concerning the dangers of Social Security: "…suppose these other businesses are themselves losing money and the government's ability to borrow or tax is therefore getting less. Under such circumstances how good is any promise of social security even the promise of government itself?"[4]

Pettengill's comments might be considered the usual partisan banter, to use today's vernacular. If you want to see something eerily prescient, take a look at this: In a 1950 study, the Chamber of Commerce of the United States predicted the very condition Ilene Davis has expressed concerns about nearly 70 years later. The Chamber's study stated, "existing welfare and security programs — Social Security, Unemployment Insurance, Workmen's Compensation, etc. — will cost 18 per cent of payrolls in a generation."[5] That prediction wasn't too far off.

The rapid expansion of the payroll tax likely came about because the original "promise" of Social Security has been greatly expanded. "Social Security was designed to help the destitute and poor, not the average person," Robert Kratzer Everett, Retirement Plan Consultant for Northeast Planning Associates, Inc. in Cambridge, Massachusetts and author of *Retirement Savings Made Simple: The 401(k)*. "At its core, it is a system that was instituted in the United States 82 years ago during the Great Depression, to help a small group of poor and elderly people by providing a supplemental amount to their other income. Today, unfortunately, it is providing the main source of income for many, if not most, retirees; therefore, it should be of no surprise with our country's demographics that expenses are greater than the inflow of new money coming into the system."

"Social Security was meant to be an aid for those who could not work due to disability or retired," says Charles Thorngren, CEO of Noble Gold Investments in Pasadena, California. "It was never designed to be the entire means to provide for oneself. When the program was started, Franklin D Roosevelt said, 'We can never insure one hundred percent of the population against one hundred percent of the hazards and vicissitudes of life… we have tried to frame a law which will give some measure of protection to the average citizen and to his family against the loss of a job and against poverty-ridden old age.'"

Roosevelt's words addressed the extreme condition many people, especially the elderly, experienced during the worst of the Depression. Joseph Gissy of Capital Management Services, located in Westlake Village, California, is a National Social Security Advisor. He says, "When Social Security was designed we had a high poverty rate for seniors coming out of the Great Depression. So, it was meant to help those in dire straits, not as the main source of retirement vehicle for all retiree's in America."

Though these views come from contemporary sources, they aren't new. Shortly after the Act's tenth anniversary, the editors of the *Buffalo Evening News* wrote, "The basic purpose of Social Security is eminently laudable. It is to provide a foundation, at or near the bare subsistence level, on which anyone can build his own economic security to his own taste by his own efforts. But the cradle-to-grave extremists have so distorted this concept that a large segment of the people have the idea that the Government has promised them not merely a foundation on which to build, but a featherbed in which to lie. The person who finds security in contemplating an old-age pittance of 67 cents a day can relax, perhaps, and let the Government do his worrying. But those with aspirations a bit loftier may find, if they take a sober look at the prospects, that there is still virtue in thrift—even in this so-called age Social Security."[6]

It's not hard to understand why Social Security is breaking. "When the program started, the average life expectancy for a man was 58 and 62 for a woman, and the benefits did not start until 65," says Michelle Morar, a financial advisor with Innovative Insurance Solutions in Greensboro, North Carolina. To put this in perspective, what would the retirement age be if the Social Security Act were to be enacted today under the same circumstances it was in 1935? In 2014, the Organization for Economic Co-operation and Development stated the average life expectancy for men and women in the United States was 76.5 and 81.3 years respectively. Give these life expectancies, the Social Security retirement age today would be 84 years.

"Social Security was never meant to last more than a few years," says Gissy. "Life expectancy in 1940 was much lower than it is today. When the program was designed we were only meant to live on it for 6 months to a year."

Morar agrees. She says "the cause of insolvency is the fact that a large percentage of our population is living well into their nineties and above. The greatest percentage of increase in an age group is the 100-year-old group. The program was not designed to sustain the amount of people who are living longer and longer."

"The population of elder, Social Security recipients continues to increase," says Brian Kulick, Wealth Management & Legacy Planner and Franchise owner of American Prosperity Group in Centreville, Virginia. "This is due to the simple fact that Americans are living longer resulting in greater cumulative benefits received by retirees than ever before. When originally designed, Social Security was not expected to provide benefits to retirees for decades. Thus, as each recipient receives more cumulative benefit that originally designed, the trust fund is exhausted more and more."

It's more than people living longer. The scope of Social Security has expanded considerably. "It's pretty simple, we have more people taking money out than we have people adding money into the system," says Gissy.

"The Social Security problem is many fold," says James R. Miller, President of Woodward Financial Advisors, Inc. in Chapel Hill, North Carolina. Besides people living much longer than expected, he points out the situation where "many people collecting off one worker's benefit (spouse, child, widow, ex-spouse, etc, and, spousal optimization strategies that may not have been expected."

So, the promise of Social Security may not yet be broke, but it's certainly in the process of breaking. "The pending insolvency isn't a surprise," says Todd Burkhalter, CEO of Drive Planning in Atlanta,

Georgia. "Basic economics says you can't spend more than you make and maintain sustainability."

While Social Security is not going "bankrupt," it's clear it will have to change in both a fundamental and disruptive way. For this reason, many financial professionals are telling their younger clients to plan on not receiving Social Security when they retire. Here's what a few of them have to say:

"It would be prudent for younger generations to plan for some adjustment to the benefit their Social Security statement is showing," says Miller. "We recommend that people in their 40s and younger assume that they'll have to wait longer to collect, will get a reduced amount (say 75% of projection) and may have to pay higher tax on Social Security benefits."

"While I hope Social Security will be there for the truly poor and destitute, I think the average person should NOT plan on Social Security being there for them for any of their retirement income in 15 to 20 years," says Everett. "I think this should be the prudent person's way of thinking about the issue."

Ilene Davis says, "Since the projected cut of 25% is expected by 2030-2035 – which is really just 12-17 years from now, anyone 50 or younger should plan for it to either not being there, or not being their ONLY source of income. I think anyone with decent savings will be cut substantially – whether through taxation or just elimination of benefits for each dollar of investment income."

"The best way to approach this is to save for retirement without factoring in any sort of monthly Social Security payment," says David Bakke, Finance Expert at Money Crashers, located in Atlanta, Georgia. "That way, if it does go broke you'll still be protected."

"I am of the belief that we should take our retirements into our own hands," says Thorngren. "With planning and some dedication, you will not need to count on the Social Security system to maintain your life in retirement. In fact, when you consider the amount of money one receives from Social Security, it by no means provides one the ability to enjoy their retirement like we all dream about. Ideally, you should take the steps to provide for yourself in retirement and remove the concern about whether Social Security will be there to help."

"I have two children," says Kulick. "One just graduated from college in May 2017 and the other is a rising sophomore in college. I have alerted both to plan for retirement assuming that Social Security will not be available for them."

Both Thorngren and Kulick express directly a form of rugged frontier self-reliance that became the backbone of early America. During that era, as we have learned, families took it upon themselves to adopt and execute intergenerational strategies to prepare for retirement. Each member, each generation, within a single family had a role and responsibility within this broader plan. Whether by design or by accident, American culture is fast returning to family-centric retirement planning. Here, the best retirement approach consists of a multi-generational design.

For example, what if Brian Kulick could have started – and finished – the process to remove his children's dependency on Social Security *before* they entered college? What if you could adopt a similar template for your own children or grandchildren? Would you be interested in learning that, by saving only $1,000 a year from the birth of your baby until that baby blows out nineteen birthday candles (plus one for good luck), you can help that baby retire a multi-millionaire?

$$*\qquad*\qquad*\qquad*\qquad*$$

That's the power of the Child IRA. That's something you can do. For some, it will appear so incredibly easy you'll kick yourself for not thinking of it. For others, you'll want to kick your parents for not thinking of it. For all, read on as we unveil the mechanics of this incredible retirement planning tool.

SECTION THREE:

– THE CHILD IRA BASICS –

EXPLAINING THE GENERAL CONCEPT

CHAPTER NINE:
IS THIS THE SOLUTION TO THE INEVITABLE
SOCIAL SECURITY CRISIS?

This may sound like an April Fools' joke, but, trust me, it's not. That's just how unbelievable it is. It's the kind of *Eureka!* discovery that can only occur in the wee small hours of the morning after endlessly toiling away at numbers and statistics and statistics and numbers.

And the beauty of it is that it works!

What if I told you there was a low cost way to wipe out the need for Social Security within one generation — and not only would it not cost the government a dime but it would generate massively more tax revenue. Would you believe me? Or would you call me an April Fool?

Most folks would bet on the latter — and most folks would be wrong!

It's so simple and obvious, it's amazing no one has ever thought of it before. Heck, it's such a great idea, I'm even willing to concede the debate on whether there's really a retirement "crisis." Here's how the idea first struck me…

It was while writing an article that is the basis for *Hey! What's My Number? – How to Improve the Odds You Will Retire in Comfort* that the idea of The Child IRA hit me like a ton of bricks.

There I was, playing with numbers in my spreadsheet models when, like a chemist whose accidental spill leads to the discovery of a fabulous cure, I inadvertently started at year 0 instead of year 15. (You'll have to read *Hey! What's My Number?* to understand the significance of starting at year 15.) Curiosity getting the better of me, rather than correcting the error, I extrapolated upon it.

Lo! And Behold! came the answer that is guaranteed to solve our nation's alleged retirement crisis. OK, OK, I said I was willing to concede the point that there really is a retirement crisis. And, admittedly so, if you consider Social Security a component of retirement, then, sooner or later, like any other Ponzi Scheme, we will find ourselves in a crisis. Only, the thing is, this idea allows Social Security to die a natural death, wiping away forever our mournful addiction to this gangster era racket.

Ready?

Here's the idea.

I'll call it "The Child IRA." It's actually something a few elite folks have taken advantage of now, assuming their children have been modeling since before they could crawl. Its effect — without the tax-deferred benefits — can also be duplicated today, mainly via trust funds, but also through regular investment accounts.

But what I'm proposing is not at all like these. It's a tax-deferred account that doesn't require earned income on the part of the primary beneficiary (i.e., the "Child" of The Child IRA). It would allow any adult (parents, grandparents or any other random unrelated adult for that matter) to contribute an aggregate total of $1,000 (pre-tax) to any child every year until they reach the age of 19. Think of it as a combination of the power of compounding found in the 401k plan with the contribution flexibility of a 529 plan.

Here's how it works. Every child born in the U. S. of A. would be allowed to accept up to $1,000 per year until their nineteenth birthday into their own "Child IRA." Any adult can make a tax-deductible contribution into anyone's Child IRA, so long as the total contributions to any single Child IRA do not exceed $1,000. The contributing adult does not have to be related to the child that owns the Child IRA.

Now, are you listening? Here's the beauty of the plan. All Child-IRAs would be required to be invested in long-term equities (preferably not through any government fund but through existing private investment vehicles like mutual funds in individual stocks). There'll be none of this "risk aversion" stuff because you can't withdraw from a Child IRA until age 70 (the "real" retirement age by the time today's kids get there). With this kind of requirement, we'd expect these Child-

IRAs to grow at the rate of return of stocks. Historically, that's a tad above 11%, but let's be conservative and say it's 8%. Do you know what that means?

That means, by contributing $1,000 a year from the year of birth until the 19th birthday (a total of $19,000 in contributions), a Child-IRA will be worth in excess of $2.2 million when the owner retires at age seventy. That's on top of any other retirement savings that person might have. And with that $2.2 million head start, where is the need for Social Security?

And what a head start it is!

The Child IRA. It's the answer to all our retirement woes. It obviates the need for Social Security (at least that part that deals with retirement). It doesn't cost the government anything to implement. Best yet, it'll leave the government with an ongoing tax windfall.

Here's how:

According to the US Census, there are roughly 75 million children in the United States. If all Child IRAs are fully funded each year, that would defer taxable income by $75 billion. Another way of saying, based on the Tax Policy Center's average Federal Tax Rate of 20.1 (for 2013, the latest year available),[1] this would equate to a short-term loss of $15 billion in revenues per year. By eerie coincidence, according to the President's 2014 budget, it costs $12.5 billion dollars to operate Social Security.[2]

But let's not get ahead of ourselves. I said this wouldn't cost anything and here's why. Looking at the costs in another way, a fully funded Child IRA ($1,000 per year until that child's nineteenth birthday) would require a total of $19,000 in total tax-deductible contributions. Again, assuming the average 20.1% tax rate, this reduces tax revenues by $201 per year for a total reduction of $3,819 over the nineteen years contributions are allowed.

By age 70, when the child retires, assuming an average annual return of 8% (versus the historic average annual return for equities of 11.17%), The Child IRA would be worth $2,267,361. Furthermore, if the retiree now takes out 4% a year ($88,506) and pays the current average tax of 20.1%, the government will earn $17,790 in tax revenues a year. That's nearly a 9,000% return on that $201 annual "investment" the government makes during the contribution period of the Child IRA. Not bad for doing nothing.

Finally, that $88,506 is 58% more than the current median income of $55,775. Traditional retirement savings vehicles will still be needed because, like Social Security, the Child IRA is not intended to fully fund retirement.

But, unlike Social Security, the Child IRA isn't a Ponzi Scheme, doesn't cost the government money (moreover, by eliminating the annual operating cost of Social Security, it'll save the government money), and, in fact, it will increase government revenues.

Like I said, it's so obviously simple, why hasn't anyone ever come up with it before? Moreover, why hasn't it already been done? I mean, we've got the 529 plan. To get to The Child IRA, all we'd have to do is say 529 plans can be used for both education (which they're currently limited to) *and* retirement. So again, why hasn't this been done already?

We'll save this answer for the book's final section (but I suspect you know the answer). For now, let's not talk about what might be done if we waited long enough for the politicians to act. Let's talk about what we could do now, by ourselves, without the need for legislation, regulatory approval, or any other third-party action. Let's dive into The Child IRA as it is today. And, believe me, you're going to want to read this because it really is as easy to do as what I just described – and just as lucrative for your children (and grandchildren).

CHAPTER TEN:
WOULD YOU MAKE THIS SACRIFICE TO HELP YOUR CHILD RETIRE A MULTI-MILLIONAIRE?

I
s it possible to eat healthy (and possibly lose weight) and achieve financial independence at the same time?

Do you regularly go out to dinner (at a real restaurant, not a fast food joint) with your special someone? If so, according to Zagat's you're probably spending about $40 a person (for a total of $80 a dinner).[1] Got a family, you say? Perhaps, in your busy schedule, you find it necessary to have your family meal at that aforementioned fast food joint (that's about $5 a head for a total of $20 a meal for a family of four). Still not striking any chords with you? How about that daily Frappuccino frenzy (about $3 a cup)?

But I digress. We're here to talk finance, not food. When thinking about retirement, people have two overriding fears: outliving their retirement savings and outlasting Social Security. If they're that worried about themselves, think how worried they'd be if they consider their children's (or grandchildren's) retirement prospects.

What if I told you there was a way to easily brush aside these fears for those children? What if I told you the solution doesn't involve fancy products, fly-by-night salesman, or too-good-to-be-true promotional pitches. Would you be interested to discover how people are already doing it? Well it's all laid out in the next several chapters. What I'm talking about is The Child IRA. Chapter 11 ("Everything You Always Wanted to Know About The Child IRA"), offers a quick recap of the concept and why it's beginning to turn a lot of heads.

The great thing about The Child IRA is people don't need to change service providers to take advantage of it. It's not a proprietary product. It doesn't require large minimum investments. In fact, it's not *just* as easy to start as a regular run-of-the-mill IRA, it *is* a regular run-of-the-mill IRA!

With one key difference, however: It's started by and for someone below the age of 18. **Well below** the age of 18. Ideally at the age of "fresh out of the oven." Although there are a number of variations to this theme (many, including "catch-up" scenarios, listed both in Chapters 11 and 20), the basic idea is this: Contribute $1,000 a year from age zero until the child's nineteenth birthday and that modest investment will grow to two-and-a-quarter million dollars by the time that child retires at age 70.

Not bad, eh? Now, I know what you're thinking: If this is such a great idea, why isn't everyone doing it? Well there are two very good reasons why we don't see Child IRAs blossoming in mutual fund accounts all across this land. First, not many people know about The Child IRA. Second, and more important, even if people are aware of The Child IRA, they aren't currently eligible to participate.

Aye, there's the rub. In order to set up The Child IRA, the child needs to have earned income. While that might be easy for a teenager, it's nigh impossible for a newborn infant. How can a new baby get a paying job? Fortunately, the wonderful world of capitalism provides reasonable access to a quick fix to this dilemma. Just turn on your favorite television show (or YouTube video channel) and, if you wait long enough, the answer will reveal itself.

As explained in Chapter 12 ("How to Take Advantage of The Child IRA Under Current Laws"), there is one job a child can do from very nearly the moment he is born: model. Baby models appear in display ads and video commercials. While the pay scale varies by market, it's not unreasonable to expect a child model to make at least the requisite $1,000 a year needed to contribute to The Child IRA. Job opportunities in top-tier markets often feature the added benefit of residuals, meaning the child can earn income in future years based on work done in a past year.

While modeling for third parties is quite competitive and demanding, there is a large market where it would be quite effortless for children to model for: their family's business. As long as parents and grandparents pay reasonable wages and stay within the applicable child labor laws, they can hire their own children to model for their business marketing materials. When children grow older, they can assume more traditional duties, as outlined in Chapter 13 ("Who is Using The Child IRA Right Now").

Naturally, a working child can generate more expenses that may offset any income. As luck would have it, the IRS only requires gross income to qualify for an IRA contribution, not net income. Therefore, even if the child's job may create an isolated negative cash flow situation, the parents' working arrangements still should net a hefty positive cash flow, making room to use the child's income to contribute to The Child IRA. If that means making sacrifices, be mindful such sacrifices aren't too burdensome. For example, $1,000 a year is equivalent to: dinner for two at a fancy restaurant once a month; or, a fast food meal for a family of four once a week; or, a single Frappuccino once a day.

Who'd have thought you could eat healthier and possibly lose weight at the same time you're helping your child gain financial independence at retirement. If all this talk about food is making you hungry to learn more about The Child IRA, the next few pages will satisfy that hunger.

CHAPTER ELEVEN:
EVERYTHING YOU ALWAYS WANTED TO KNOW ABOUT THE CHILD IRA

Beginning in the winter of 2014, a series of articles came out that represent the beginnings of a concept called "The Child IRA." The following chapters will answer the most asked questions about The Child IRA. First, I'll briefly explain the numbers behind what makes The Child IRA so attractive and some variations that allow it to be replicated. (For those more inclined, Chapter 14 takes you deeper into how the numbers work.) Next, we'll explore what's required to create and contribute to The Child IRA under current laws, including why those variations may be more realistic than the original concept of contributing $1,000 a year for nineteen years. Finally, we'll review some real-world examples of The Child IRA in action, including a twist that you might have overlooked.

Summary of The Child IRA

The genesis of The Child IRA began with the article "What Every 401k Plan Sponsor and Fiduciary Should Disclose to Employees: How to Retire a Millionaire (Hint: It's Easier Than You Think)," (*FiduciaryNews.com*, February 25, 2014). This piece discussed an approach commonly used in 401k education sessions to persuade employees to begin saving as early as possible. It compares a 15-year old saving $1,000 a year for sixteen years vs. a 40-year old saving $5,000 for the same time period. Assuming they each retire at age 70, the younger saver finds he has nearly three-quarters of a million dollars while the older saver has only a little more than half a million dollars. This despite the 40-year old saves five times more than the 15-year old.

A spreadsheet accident led to a follow-up article, the first to mention the phrase "The Child IRA." In the course of running the numbers of the first article, the age was inadvertently reset to zero instead of fifteen. The almost penicillin-like serendipity led to the publication of the article "This idea will solve the retirement crisis, guaranteed!?" (*BenefitsPro*, February 26, 2014). By dialing back the start age from "age 15" to "new born baby" and investing that $1,000 annually until said baby reaches age 19, we find the value of The Child IRA will have grown to two-and-a-quarter million dollars. That's right. For the price of a $19,000 investment, the "child" in The Child IRA becomes a multi-millionaire when retirement hits at age 70. Said another way, for about the cost of dinner for two each month, or the cost of a family meal at McDonald's once a week, or less than the cost of that daily Vanilla Bean Crème Frappuccino at Starbucks, parents can help set their child on the path to a quite comfortable retirement. (But if you remembered what you read in the previous chapter you'd already know this, which, by the way, is the point of the repetition you see repeatedly in this section of the book.)

With that in mind, it quickly became apparent The Child IRA could easily obviate the need for Social Security. "It's time we create a Child IRA," *Benefit Selling*, April 2014) explains, in numerical detail, how The Child IRA can become a viable national policy to eventually replace Social Security. Finally, the entire notion of The Child IRA was fleshed out and repurposed to become Appendix V in the book *Hey! What's My Number? – How to Improve The Odds You Will Retire in Comfort*, (Christopher Carosa, 2014, Pandamensional Solutions). But, enough of the history lesson. What you really want to know is "What makes The Child IRA tick?"

About the Assumptions Used with The Child IRA

The first major assumption is the return assumption used in the 70-year period encompassing The Child IRA. The number used is 8%. This is roughly 3% less than the 11.04% median return for the nineteen 70-year rolling periods from 1928 through 2015 (based on the Stern-NYU annual return data for the S&P 500). Moreover, it is more than 2% less than the worst performing 70-year rolling period (10.40%). This cushion is more than enough to incorporate account fees, timing of cash flows, and sequence of return risk.

Despite the conservative nature of the return assumption, it's best to view the $2.2 million end result as a good "approximation." It's also important to remember this retirement fund does not include retirement savings made by the child during their working adult years. As Chapter 9 concludes, it's a great "head start."

The second major assumption deals with the $1,000 annual contribution. This begins from the year the baby is born and ends when that child turns nineteen. There are two important considerations with this assumption. First, in the real world, given the opportunity most would maximize the annual contribution (currently $5,500) and not limit themselves to only a fraction of that. The $1,000 annual contribution used in our example is meant to show how easy it would be to establish and maintain The Child IRA. In addition, it demonstrates how a small sacrifice (one Frappuccino a day) can yield a return of huge magnitude (to the tune of two-and-a-quarter million).

As we'll learn in the next chapter, several obstacles stand in the way before one can take advantage of The Child IRA. For one, it applies only to new born babies. But, can older children also avail themselves of The Child IRA? The quick answer is "yes." This is the benefit of not relying on the maximum available contribution. In fact, as Chart I. "Catching Up to The Child IRA" illustrates, the entire shortfall can be made up in the first year's contribution up until age 4. Indeed, by utilizing the annual maximum, one can "catch-up" by starting at any age up to and including age 12. Once you start at ages 13 and older, you'll need to make contributions beyond age 18. For example, to achieve the same end result when starting at age 18, you'll need to contribute the maximum $5,500 until age 27 and then another $3,434 at age 28.

CHART I. "CATCHING UP TO THE CHILD IRA"
(ANNUAL CONTRIBUTION RATES TO YIELD THE SAME RESULT AT AGE 70)

Age:	New Born	Age 1	Age 2	Age 3	Age 4	Age 5	Age 6	Age 7	Age 8	Age 9	Age 10	Age 11	Age 12	Age 13	Age 14	Age 15	Age 16	Age 17	Age 18	Age 19	Age 20	Age 21	Age 22
0	1,000																						
1	1,000	2,099																					
2	1,000	1,000	3,246																				
3	1,000	1,000	1,000	4,506																			
4	1,000	1,000	1,000	1,000	5,500																		
5	1,000	1,000	1,000	1,000	1,396	5,500																	
6	1,000	1,000	1,000	1,000	1,000	2,989	5,500																
7	1,000	1,000	1,000	1,000	1,000	1,000	4,697	5,500															
8	1,000	1,000	1,000	1,000	1,000	1,000	1,000	2,132	5,500														
9	1,000	1,000	1,000	1,000	1,000	1,000	1,000	1,000	4,291	5,500													
10	1,000	1,000	1,000	1,000	1,000	1,000	1,000	1,000	1,000	2,213	5,500												
11	1,000	1,000	1,000	1,000	1,000	1,000	1,000	1,000	1,000	1,000	4,933	5,500											
12	1,000	1,000	1,000	1,000	1,000	1,000	1,000	1,000	1,000	1,000	1,000	2,605	5,500										
13	1,000	1,000	1,000	1,000	1,000	1,000	1,000	1,000	1,000	1,000	1,000	1,000	5,500	5,500									
14	1,000	1,000	1,000	1,000	1,000	1,000	1,000	1,000	1,000	1,000	1,000	1,000	5,500	5,500	5,500								
15	1,000	1,000	1,000	1,000	1,000	1,000	1,000	1,000	1,000	1,000	1,000	1,000	5,500	5,500	5,500	5,500							
16	1,000	1,000	1,000	1,000	1,000	1,000	1,000	1,000	1,000	1,000	1,000	1,000	3,560	5,500	5,500	5,500	5,500						
17	1,000	1,000	1,000	1,000	1,000	1,000	1,000	1,000	1,000	1,000	1,000	1,000	5,500	5,500	5,500	5,500	5,500	5,500					
18	1,000	1,000	1,000	1,000	1,000	1,000	1,000	1,000	1,000	1,000	1,000	1,000	1,183	5,500	5,500	5,500	5,500	5,500	5,500				
19	1,000	1,000	1,000	1,000	1,000	1,000	1,000	1,000	1,000	1,000	1,000	1,000	5,500	4,770	5,500	5,500	5,500	5,500	5,500	5,500			
20	1,000	1,000	1,000	1,000	1,000	1,000	1,000	1,000	1,000	1,000	1,000	1,000	5,500	5,500	3,389	5,500	5,500	5,500	5,500	5,500	5,500		
21	1,000	1,000	1,000	1,000	1,000	1,000	1,000	1,000	1,000	1,000	1,000	1,000	5,500	5,500	5,500	2,592	5,500	5,500	5,500	5,500	5,500	5,500	
22	1,000	1,000	1,000	1,000	1,000	1,000	1,000	1,000	1,000	1,000	1,000	1,000	5,500	5,500	5,500	5,500	2,542	5,500	5,500	5,500	5,500	5,500	5,500
23														5,500	5,500	5,500	5,500	3,434	5,500	5,500	5,500	5,500	5,500
24														5,500	5,500	5,500	5,500	5,500	3,799	5,500	5,500	5,500	5,500
25														5,500	5,500	5,500	5,500	5,500	5,500	4,345	5,500	5,500	5,500
26															5,500	5,500	5,500	5,500	5,500	5,500	2,881	5,500	5,500
27																5,500	5,500	5,500	5,500	5,500	5,500		5,500
28																	5,500	5,500	5,500	5,500	5,500		
29																		5,500	5,500	5,500	5,500		
30																			5,500	5,500	5,500		
31																				5,500	5,500		
32																					5,500		
33																					5,500		
34																					4,345		
35																					5,500		
36																					5,500		
37																					5,500		
38																					5,500		
39																					5,500		
40																					2,881		

The Child IRA for College Aged Children?

The Child IRA also works for college aged children, (although by that age, The Child IRA is nothing more than a regular IRA). We won't dwell too much on this because the circumstances have been addressed many times before as justification for starting an IRA. For the purposes of comparative continuity, however, we'll share with you the numbers in terms of achieving the same results as The Child IRA. For example, to reap the same $2.2 million reward as The Child IRA, a 19-year who begins saving $5,500 a year must contribute that same amount through age 30. If the college student waits until age 22 to start, maximum contributions must be made every year until age 39, then another $2,881 must be made at age 40.

At the very least, The Child IRA for college aged children validates the power of compounding. But we're looking at starting The Child IRA when children are infants. There aren't many ways for these tiny tots to earn an income. The next chapter gives you a quick summary of one of the best ways to do this.

CHAPTER TWELVE:
HOW TO TAKE ADVANTAGE OF THE CHILD IRA UNDER CURRENT TAX LAWS

Now that you know everything you need to know about the concept of The Child IRA, let's learn what it takes to benefit from The Child IRA. Remember, the one significant drawback of The Child IRA is that, under current laws, it can't be utilized unless the child has earned income. Since the full value of The Child IRA assumes IRA contributions begin the first year a child is born, it requires that newborn to have a job. There aren't many jobs newborns can take. But there are some. Let's explore them.

The Best Way For Newborns to Begin Using The Child IRA

Newborn babies have limited skills. They can breathe, they can eat, they can... well you can figure out the rest. There are plenty of things they can't do. They can't answer the telephone. They can't file alphabetically. They haven't even mastered simple tools like Microsoft Office, let alone advanced tools like Adobe's Creative Cloud. In fact, they're only capable of doing one thing: existing.

The world offers precious few jobs that require only existence, but that newborn baby will have to find those jobs and then convince an employer to hire him (i.e., that newborn baby) in order to earn the necessary income to start a Child IRA. What kinds of jobs require one to merely sit there and do nothing? Pretty much only one: modeling. Think of all those (practically) newborn babies acting in all those diaper commercials, insurance commercials, and just about any other type of advertising (both still and video). Those babies don't work for free, either. They all get paid. For them, The Child IRA is more than just a philosophical idea, it's a practical tool.

For many, landing a job as a modeling professional seems far-fetched, if not impossible. Certainly, they think, such positions are available only to those with connections, not for the common folk. Just like any other job, it's not as hard to get if you're willing to do what's necessary. "Breaking into the business is not difficult at all," says Kent Friel, Executive Director at the Mary Therese Friel Modeling Agency in Mendon, New York. "A parent interested in getting their child into modeling should research potential agencies and look for a reputable company with a proven track record to get involved with. An agency like ours will help guide you through the process and help you learn the business."

What precisely does it mean to be a model and what are the kinds of jobs one can expect when modeling? "The type of modeling work we are discussing here is commercial print work and television commercials," says Friel. "Typically, models in these types of bookings are seen in advertising images placed in print publications, on television, and in electronic media. There is other modeling work available like fashion/runway and television/film acting. They all have different payment rates associated with them."

How Much Can a Child Model Expect to Earn?

The first step is landing the gig. Next, the child must earn enough to start and maintain annual contributions in The Child IRA. Recall our hurdle is low because The Child IRA is predicated on contributing only $1,000 a year (or perhaps more the first few years if the child doesn't start working as a newborn infant). Is it reasonable to expect the child to earn the minimum necessary to continually fund The Child IRA? Friel says, "The question is difficult to answer because the range of compensation for child models is varied. Every booking is different, every client is different and every model is different. Like any job, compensation rates are tied to qualifications, in many cases. The more training and experience a model has, the higher the rate they can command on a booking. Additionally, compensation for a modeling booking tends to increase based on the geographical area that an ad will be shown in (local, regional, national, etc.). This factor is usually in line with the size of the company producing the ad."

Getting the actual job is only the first hurdle. The next involves earning enough money to cover the minimum annual contribution of The Child IRA. Friel divides the modeling market into three geographic tiers. "In a third-tier market like Rochester, New York," says Friel, "a child can earn approximately $50 - $150 per hour, or $500 to $1000 per day. Most of the work is local and regional in scale. Because the child model is working in their hometown, parents have the added advantage of preserving the child's normal schedule and do not have to travel for auditions and bookings." This translates into working between seven and twenty hours a year in smaller markets to generate the minimum annual contribution of $1,000.

Larger markets offer higher paydays, making it easier not only to fund the minimum, but to fund the full maximum allowable annual contribution. This may be an important factor for children who haven't started modeling as newborns to make catch-up contributions to The Child IRA. "Second-tier markets like Chicago, Philadelphia and Miami offer much regional and national work for models," says Friel. "This work pays a higher rate for the job than the third-tier markets. Top-tier markets like New York City and Los Angeles offer national bookings for network TV and pay the best rates. Models receive a standard appearance fee for the shoot and a residual fee based on the amount of air time the commercial receives. These commercials would be for national brands. Sustaining ongoing work of this nature requires joining a union (SAG/AFTRA) and being able to either travel to these cities on a regular basis, or relocate."

Can a Child Sustain a Modeling Career From Infancy Through Early Adulthood?

In order to take full advantage of The Child IRA, the child will need to contribute $1,000 a year for nineteen years (from ages 0 through age 18). Is it reasonable to expect a child's modeling career to last that long? After all, someone who's cute as a three-year old might not make the cut once the body starts changing during adolescence. "At our agency, we represent professional models from infancy through the senior years," says Friel. "We have been in business for 30 years and have models still working with us today who started their modeling careers with us when they were children. Theoretically, a person could begin modeling as a newborn and continue through all of their growing years and into their adult years."

But it's more than natural looks and talent that keep child models employed. Friel says, "This is a job that you have to possess a drive and determination to be involved in for the long term. It looks easy to observers, because it is supposed to appear that way. The reality is that much training, preparation and auditioning happens before any work is booked. The work is truly fun and rewarding."

More important, a successful child modeling career requires a support group well beyond the child's ability to control and manage. "To be successful," says Friel, "child models need representation, professional photos, and training. They also need a parent or guardian who has the time to accompany the child to all of their modeling activities."

In short, a child's modeling career may last only so long for any number of reasons. Friel says, "Modeling careers for children end because one or more of these ingredients is missing. For example, an agency will represent a model for as long as they deem that the model is marketable, which means that the model has the physical attributes and professional acumen that the agency desires. If a model doesn't have photos that accurately show their current look, it is impossible for an agent to promote them for opportunities. As the child model ages, if they don't seek training opportunities, they won't develop the necessary skill base they need for the business."

While the actual working years may be limited, the earning years can be extended if the jobs entail residuals. Depending on the nature of the work, these residuals can last for years, allowing the child to continue to contribute to The Child IRA long after the working days have finished.

Of course, there's another way to look at this. Suppose (as is often the case), a newborn baby has "that perfect look" for one-time ad placements and earns several thousand dollars (or at least $5,500 a year). It's not unusual for a newborn's looks and demeanor to change as to make them unemployable (can anyone say "terrible twos"?). Let's take the case where the newborn is only actively working for the first two years and does not make any residuals. If the newborn contributes the maximum ($5,500 a year) to The Child IRA for those two years, the amount The Child IRA will grow to when that child reaches age 70 will be very nearly the same (actually, a tad bit more) compared to a Child IRA that is funded at $1,000 a year from age 0 through age 18. So, just because a modeling career is short doesn't mean the child can't experience the full benefits of The Child IRA.

Chapter 19 takes a deeper look at child modeling and child acting, and some of the pitfalls of taking this route, including one very famous one.

Special Case: The Parents Own a Business

The modeling profession is highly competitive. It requires a lot of dedication and hard work to sustain a career. But there may be a way to cut corners. Parents who own businesses and actively advertise represent a special situation. In this situation, maintaining a steady stream of child modeling work may demand less rigor. "A parent of a child model can provide regular and predictable bookings for the model in the advertising that they produce for their own company," says Friel. "This situation also provides control over the child's modeling career as well, which is completely absent when the model is working for other companies."

Still, it's important for the parents to continue to do things by the book. This includes not only offering fair compensation that is justified by the amount of work completed, but also to stay within the confines of any applicable child labor laws. For example, Friel says, "In New York State it is important to run bookings like this through a professional agency, like ours, with the proper permits to maintain compliance with the Department of Labor Child Performer laws." Chapter 18 explores this option in more detail.

Are You Interested in Utilizing The Child IRA This Way?

Current or prospective parents and grandparents may be interested in looking into child modeling as a way for their children and grandchildren to generate the earnings necessary to take advantage of The Child IRA. How would they go about doing this? "Take the time to do your own research to find a reputable agency that you can trust," says Friel. "Expect to pay for your own expenses (photos, training, etc.). There is a lot of information available that says models do not need to pay for anything. The reality is that if you don't pay for them on your own, the agency will assign the cost to your 'book' and you will end up paying for these expenses, plus interest, from your bookings, or at the end of your contract if the expenses were not earned."

Not everyone is cut out to be a model. More people don't even see this as a realistic option. They instead chose a more traditional route. The next chapter provides a few examples of how they did (and maybe how you can do it, too).

CHAPTER THIRTEEN:
WHO IS USING THE CHILD IRA RIGHT NOW?

The previous chapter discussed one way to fund The Child IRA. The good news, we learned the most obvious way (once you realize it) for children to earn income from virtually the moment they're born. "Under the age of 5," says Ira Smilovitz, Enrolled Agent and owner of Glenwood Tax Services in Leonia, New Jersey, "the typical job is as a child actor/model. Earnings can be anything from a few hundred dollars to many thousands."

The bad news: we also learned this ideal approach requires much advance planning and almost immediate action. For many, we are well past this stage in the child's life. Rest assured, though, mentioned earlier, children well into their elementary school years can still avail themselves to The Child IRA. Beyond infancy, paid prospects begin to broaden. Saul Simon, financial advisor with Lincoln Financial and President of Simon Financial Group in Edison, New Jersey says, depending on the child's age, employment opportunities can range from "pictures for marketing promotion, filing, cleaning, and sweeping." Besides using the income to fund The Child IRA, getting a job helps the child by "teaching responsibility and money values," says Simon.

Once a child moves from celebrating kindergarten graduation and heads into the pre-teen years, we start to see more traditional work become available. Rocky Lalvani, Enrolled Agent and Financial Coach located in the Harrisburg, Pennsylvania Area says regarding the ages between 6 and 12, "at the upper end of this would be babysitting, yard work, and other household chores. They could also help setting up technology. Because of their age the wages will naturally be very low."

Be warned, however, since paying children for working around the house may garner the attention of regulators. "The children's ages can vary and their duties and pay will vary accordingly," says Sean Moore, President of SMART College Funding in Boca Raton, Florida. "The pay needs to be commensurate with the work performed, and both must be reasonable. Paying your 8-year old $30 per hour to take out the trash not only sets unreasonable expectations about the value of a dollar, it may also raise eyebrows at the IRS. While small children will probably get paid at or near minimum wage, older kids may prove to be far more valuable to the company and paid handsomely."

Upon reaching the teen years, all those years of technological immersion – yes, that includes video games – can begin to pay off. "Most of the work is now social media driven because young kids know platforms such as Instagram, Facebook, and Snapchat better than their parents and for the cost can do a really good job in helping an owner brand their business," says Ted Jenkin, Co-CEO and Founder at oXYGen Financial in Atlanta, Georgia. "Otherwise, children are limited to mostly menial day to day labor type tasks. You must pay the kids what would be considered to be fair compensation for that job if you were to hire someone out in the open marketplace – $12 to $18 an hour depending on age and skill. The most important thing is to have the job fully documented and set up an HR file for your child."

More appropriately, rather than paying for housework, it may make more sense – and have its own set of additional advantages – for parents and grandparents who own their own businesses to hire their family descendants. "I know parents that hire their children," says Moore. "In fact, I actively recommend that business owner parents hire their children and then use some (or all) of the proceeds to fund an IRA."

Earning enough money to fund The Child IRA helps the child, but do you know hiring their child can also help the business owner. Edward R. Collins, Founding Partner & Wealth Advisor at Artisan Wealth Management, LLC in Lebanon, New Jersey calls it "a dramatically underutilized tax savings strategy to hire younger family members and put them on the books. Most business owners don't realize that there is no requirement to withhold the traditional payroll taxes (FUTA, SUTA, FICA, etc.) when paying ones' own children under the age of 18, so long as the business is a sole proprietorship or a partnership in which each partner is a parent of the child. Even though this benefit goes away if the business is a corporation or includes partners who are not a parent of the child employee, almost every state allows for the child employee to be waived out of Worker's Compensation coverage if they are covered under the family medical plan of the business owner."

Besides payroll taxes, there may be income tax benefits. "Depending on the income you actually pay to the young family member, and depending on whether or not they file their own income tax return, there may be no income tax liability regardless of the funding of a retirement plan," says Collins. "Every person who files an income tax return is eligible for the Personal Exemption and the Standard Deduction. For 2016, the Personal Exemption is $4,050. The Standard Deduction is $6,300 this year. When I am suggesting this strategy I typically focus on children under the age of 18. They often do part-time work – clerical or general administrative. It needs to be at least just enough from a legitimate compensation perspective to meet the IRS earned income requirement. It is extremely important to note that taxes are a complicated animal. Before implementing any strategy, one should consult with a qualified financial professional to ensure they are coloring within the lines with the IRS."

Once the necessary income is earned, the next task is to determine which form of IRA should be used for The Child IRA. "In nearly all scenarios," says Moore, "I recommend using a Roth IRA. Because most children's income will be less than the standard deduction, the Roth IRA is a perfect fit. It allows for tax-deferred growth, tax-free withdrawals of contributions at any time, penalty free withdrawals of earnings for college expenses and tax-free withdrawals upon retirement. Some families are just starting to take advantage of this strategy while others have been doing it for 5 years or longer."

Bob Chitrathorn, Vice President of Wealth Planning/Senior at Trilogy Financial in Corona, California, agrees with Moore. He says parents "are using Roth IRA's and have been doing them for a few years."

Remember, with The Child IRA, the child only needs to earn the money. That money could be spent on other items and the actual contribution can come from any source. "Often the parents will gift the IRA contribution," says Smilovitz. "In other words, if the child earns $1,000, the parent(s) gift $1,000 to the child to fund the Roth IRA and let the child keep the earnings to use as the child wishes (subject to parental approval)."

Real-Life Stories

What follows is a compilation of several real-life examples of The Child IRA in use. Parents and grandparents expecting a new addition to their families might be mindful of these stories, especially if they own a small business.

Benjamin L. Grosz, a benefits and tax attorney at Ivins, Phillips & Barker in Washington, DC, says, "I know a business owner who hires his nieces/nephews (he has no children of his own) and has coordinated with their parents to use the funds to set up Roth IRAs for the children. They have been contributing to them for a number of years. The children were first hired when the youngest was quite young (age two, I think). They have been employed as models, and paid in line with industry norms."

"I know half a dozen – maybe more – real estate investors who do this," says Don Tepper, Owner of Solutions 3D, LLC in Fairfax, Virginia. "Most of the children are now age 10 or greater. The type of work they do includes envelope addressing, postcard addressing, stuffing letters into envelopes, applying stamps to envelopes, and sealing them. (Basically, different elements of direct mail campaigns.) The pay range is between $7-$15 per hour. They have been contributing since the child/children were old enough to perform some sort of useful work – in a few cases that I know about, around ages 6 or 7."

Of course, it's not surprising that financial advisers themselves have taken advantage of The Child IRA. "I was able to give my kids '$200,000' this past Christmas in their retirement account," says

Lalvani. "I did this, making sure they had earned income and then figuring out the best retirement account to put it in. It's hard for younger kids to earn an income and if the IRS thinks it's not reasonable you may run afoul of them. Laws make it hard to work for someone else."

Smart parents have long known of the concept of The Child IRA. Here's a testimonial from someone whose father used The Child IRA two decades ago. "My father did this for me when I was 12 or so," says Erin Kelley, Founder & CEO of Collizio, Inc. in Washington, DC. "I did clerical work (filing, mailing, etc.), and I was paid $7 an hour. I worked enough to maximize the contribution. We used a Roth IRA. I still have it, 20 years later, though I used some of the contributions to pay for graduate school."

Kelley exposes one of the drawbacks of using a Roth version of an IRA for The Child IRA. Since one can withdraw from a Roth without consequences after five years, there may be a temptation to use that money to pay for expenses other than retirement.

Casey St. Henry, Financial Associate at Thrivent Financial Ellison Bay, Wisconsin says, "I work with a number of small business owners who employ their children and use their earnings to fund a Roth IRA on the kids' behalf. They tend to choose the Roth account for the tax-free withdrawals to help fund their children's education. The folks I'm familiar with all have children in the 6 – 14 age range, and they do a number of different tasks. One of my colleagues has his five children clean the offices of his business. They go in every Sunday after church and get their work done. Another family that I work with owns a restaurant, and their three kids do everything from salad prep in the kitchen to bussing tables to hosting and working as wait staff during the slow times. I don't know their actual pay range, but all of them work pretty much year-round, and come close to maxing out their Roth accounts at $5,500 per year. I find that the amount of time that they've been using this strategy depends on how early they have been made aware of the possibility and the risks inherent in the workplace. Many of the people I work with have low-danger businesses, so the kids can start young, doing menial tasks, without much risk of injury."

"The Child IRA" may represent a recent name for something that a few forward thinking people have been employing for some time. It's a retirement savings tool that has been far too underutilized. Granted, regulators have not made it easy for children to start their own IRA. For instance, it might be easier if, like the popular 529 college savings account, the IRA contribution rules were changed to allow parents, grandparents, or any other adult for that matter to fund Child IRA contributions out of the donor's earnings rather than require the child to have earnings. Still, that there are a number of Child IRAs currently in existence attests to the usefulness of this idea.

In the next section, we'll begin with a much more complete story of how one family started IRAs for their children. Then we'll explore each of the areas touched in this section in much greater detail. Unlike the preceding chapters, which are meant to be an overview on The Child IRA, the following chapters contain the nuts and bolts of what you must do to establish a Child IRA.

SECTION FOUR:

– THE PRACTICAL CHILD IRA –

A SPECIFIC GUIDE TO ESTABLISH A CHILD IRA FOR YOUR CHILDREN AND GRANDCHILDREN

CHAPTER FOURTEEN:
A FAMILY THAT SAVES TOGETHER...

It was the late 1990s. The stock market was booming, riding the wave of dot-com enthusiasm. Amy Bernstein was working as an attorney for the wealth management area of Harris Bank in Chicago. One day, while skimming through "a 'retail' magazine or website," she happened upon an article describing the benefits of setting up an IRA for a minor child. Amy discussed the idea with her husband Bob, who was a manager at the Academic Computer Center at the University of Illinois at Chicago. The two decided the article made sense.

As Amy and Bob were salaried employees working for big firms, they decided to wait until their children were old enough to work. Because neither had been operating a family business, they realized they couldn't hire their kids to do work for them and, at the time, Amy didn't want to mess around trying to document babysitting jobs.

Jennifer, their oldest, was very good with managing her day to day expenses. (One thing Amy and Bob did with both their kids was give them a clothing allowance in their teens.) When she was old enough to work, Jennifer got her first in a long series of typical jobs kids her age have had. She worked as a camp counselor, a grocery store cashier, and taught ice skating for the park district. Jennifer didn't show a whole lot of interest in investments, but she understood the benefit of saving and, especially, of saving early. Despite this understanding, she never really showed an interest in managing money in terms of investments.

When that first outside income came in, Amy sat down with Jennifer to discuss the idea of establishing a Roth IRA with her teenage earnings. "I have a vague recollection of my mom telling me that she was setting up a Roth IRA for me when I was in high school," recalls Jennifer today. "My parents have always been small "C" conservative with money – they have saved first and spent second – and so the news that my mom was creating some sort of savings vehicle for me wasn't really surprising."

Jennifer let her mom do everything. "She told me what she was doing, she wanted me to be informed, but she knew if she left it up to me at age 16 it wouldn't get done – at most I might have signed some papers." So Amy opened up a Roth IRA for Jennifer at Harris Bank when she was a senior in high school from the $593 Jennifer earned that fall as a cashier and ice skating teacher.

Amy remembers, "The interest rate was a whole .79%. It stayed in the savings account until March of 2002 when I had her roll it over to Vanguard. At that time, we made a $2000 gift to her to add to the IRA, based on her earnings for 2001, which included the spring of her senior high school year (cashier and skating instructor) and summer camp counselor. At that point, it went into a money market fund (don't ask me why). I think I wanted her to get involved in investment decisions and she wasn't really interested so I just opted for something that would be safe."

Amy and Bob's son Andrew, on the other hand, had long been interested in investments. "I don't really know what got Andrew interested," says Amy. "But as you can see from Jen's story, it wasn't because she was interested in investing. Andrew, on the other hand, was interested in all things related to money." When he was 9-years-old, Andrew got the chief investment officer of Harris Bank to invest five dollars for him. Andrew celebrated his 16th birthday in 2006 and began working (as a camp counselor, camp director and soccer coach). As part of helping him set up his own Roth IRA, Amy had the "talk" with him. "It definitely added to his already existing interest," recalls Amy, "he even opened a brokerage account when he was 18 and invested in stocks with his earnings."

From Andrew's perspective, his mother's idea fascinated him. "I remember feeling intrigued," says Andrew. "My mom explained the concept thoroughly and I understood that the money being put away now would be there for me when I retired. She explained that the money would generate interest, which meant that the money would make more money. She also made sure I understood that I shouldn't ever touch the money in my Roth IRA until retirement because I would lose out on a lot of money if I did that."

In February 2007, when Andrew was 16, Amy opened a Roth IRA for him. It was initially funded with the $349 he had earned the previous tax year. Two $1,000 contributions were added that fall. Even though Andrew earned this money, he was able to spend it on other things as his parents gifted the contributions used to fund his IRA.

Jennifer and Andrew also had jobs in college during the year and summers, including tutoring Hebrew, working as a camp counselor, working as a dorm resident advisor and working as a travel coordinator for an international youth exchange program. "I let them keep the money they earned and made the contributions myself as gifts to them and put in the maximum of eligible earned income," says Amy.

While both Jennifer and Andrew continued to contribute to their IRA through college, the two children approached their IRA differently. Jennifer let her mom handle it while Andrew took a more active role. (In addition to his IRA, he set up an E*Trade account for trading stocks and mutual funds.)

There was an additional major difference between Andrew's IRA savings and Jennifer's. Given Andrew's interest in investments, his IRA was immediately invested in a stock fund. "We put his money straight into a stock fund, the Scout International Fund which was then managed by UMB," says Amy.

Today, both of Amy and Bob's children are productive adults. Jennifer (34) and Andrew (26), are both very happy to have the nest egg. Outside of their IRAs, Jennifer, who is a foreign service officer, is also making substantial contributions to her federal thrift savings plan account. Andrew, who teaches in a charter school in Memphis and seems to work more than 24 hours a day, has a small 401k, in addition to his state pension plan. Amy says, "I attribute their saving for retirement on their own in employer sponsored programs to the fact that they have seen the benefits of investing at a young age through their IRAs, plus the example my husband and I have set, putting aside the maximum allowable for retirement over the years." Though both of their children have good jobs, Amy and Bob still make annual gifts to them to cover at least part of their retirement savings.

Now, nearly twenty years after first discovering the benefits of establishing the IRAs for the children, the entire family sees the benefit and is glad to have done it. Her husband credits Amy with driving the whole idea from the outset. "Amy is way better at recognizing and acting on issues like this proactively," says Bob. "She is really, really good at taking a conservative, long-term approach to financial planning and acting on it. Not just IRAs for the kids, but our own pensions, savings for colleges, investing in a house, and so forth."

While pleased with heeding the advice of that article she read two decades ago, in retrospect, Amy does have a couple regrets. "I think," she says, "I would have tried to find a way to document babysitting jobs, etc… before they turned sixteen to start the Roth IRAs sooner." In addition, at least in terms of Jennifer's IRA, Amy wishes she had invested for the long-term rather than safety. "I should have been in stocks for her right from the start," she says, "but given her lack of interest and my conservatism, we missed a significant opportunity along the way. That being said, at least the money was saved!"

For Jennifer, the experience has been both beneficial and eye-opening. She says, "I don't think I totally grasped the benefit of having a Roth IRA started before I personally could afford to pay into it, because I've never been hugely fascinated by finances – I think a general understanding is necessary but I'm fiscally risk-averse and I'm not drawn to investing. But I got the concept of compound interest so it sounded like a good (and generous) idea. Now, understanding more about savings and finances, it's an even better and more generous idea. My family tends to live long (a grandfather died at 99 and my other grandfather will turn 99 this December) so the amount of money I'll need to save will be considerable, which can only happen through compound interest over decades."

Andrew, the more aggressive investor, seems delighted with the way things have turned out. "I've learned that the earlier you start saving, the higher returns you will have over the course of 30-40 years," he says. "It also peaked my interest in other investment vehicles. I love having a retirement vehicle that typically generates a healthy return every year. I feel secure in knowing that I have over $20,000 in a Roth IRA at the age of 26 that will provide a nest egg for when I retire in addition to my teachers pension and other savings. I feel fortunate that my mom had the foresight to set it up for me and contribute over the years."

Amy continues to be proactive, only now it's on behalf of others. "I have been preaching setting up Roth IRAs for kids to lots of people," she says. "They find it interesting but I don't think anyone has done it. I'm not sure if it is because they don't have the excess cash or it just seems too strange. You do have to have confidence that your kids won't take it out when it is under their control, just like if you use an UTMA account."

While Jennifer hasn't yet had the opportunity to share the good news of her experience "because I'm not asked," she isn't afraid to offer it. "I think parents most often talk to other parents about child issues, and finances are always a tricky topic for Americans to discuss," she says, "But I would if asked."

Andrew, on the other hand, appears to have been put in the position of being asked plenty of times. "I have fielded a lot of questions from friends about financial planning," he says. "My advice is always the same: once you build up a savings account that covers 4-6 months of expenses open a Roth IRA. Take care of the immediate, then the long term, then invest in medium term."

As for the future, there's no question about it, Andrew would do the same thing for his children what his mother and father did for him. The school teacher says, "The benefits of starting to invest money that will yield interest for 50+ years is the smartest thing you can do for your kids besides paying high property taxes for access to excellent teachers and saving for college so your kids can graduate debt free."

Chapter Fifteen:
How the Numbers Work

Remember when you were a little kid and you fell and you scraped your knee? It hurt bad and it seemed like the pain would never go away. If you were really young you probably cried and cried. Pitying you, your mother would come up to you, give you a loving hug, and say, "Yes, I know it hurts now, but the pain will eventually go away." And, you know what? Your mother was right.

Time may heal all wounds, but it does something else. The passage of time insulates us from our worse fears. One of the greatest fears we innately possess is the fear of the future. Well, it's not exactly a fear of the future, it is the fear associated with uncertainty.

Let me give you an example. After more than three decades (or more if you count my teenage ventures) of business and entrepreneurial experience, I can look back and confidently say, "That was easy." With the benefit of the rearview mirror, I can clearly see how all the dots are connected. Building a sustaining business – no matter what market that business caters to – seems to me a straightforward process. Even looking ahead in planning the future, the benefit of this veteran template allows me to reduce uncertainty dramatically. (People often say I'm not afraid of risk because I've started so many businesses from scratch. I tell them the truth is quite the opposite. I am risk-averse. Before I begin a new project, I try to identify and mitigate as many risk factors as possible.)

With this mindset in mind, I got to thinking. I figured if I could consistently build sustainable businesses, anybody else could. All they needed was a variation of the template I've been using. So I approached my daughter, a recent college graduate, with the idea. It wasn't for her, as she has a career track in mind. It was more for her peers. When I suggested people her age didn't need to worry, they just needed to follow this template, her response hit me like a slap in the face.

"Dad," she said, "you're looking at this with the benefit of hindsight. You see a road behind you that you have already travelled. People my age see a road ahead, and they have no way of knowing what's coming around the bend."

Uncertainty. It's not the fear of the future, it's the fear of the uncertainty that comes with the future. The future represents a fork with many roads to choose from. And above this fork of many roads hovers the ominous cloud of uncertainty. Which is the best road to take? Not even Robert Frost can give you the correct answer.

In fact, the farther ahead you look, the darker that cloud of uncertainty becomes. When we talk of The Child IRA, we're talking about a time span of 70 years. Yes, seventy years is a very long time, but remember, time heals all wounds.

In this case, it's not wounds we seek to heal, but uncertainty we wish to reduce. Long time frames accomplish this by smoothing an otherwise bumpy road. We see this with the average annual return of stocks. From 1926 through 2016, the median annual one-year return for stocks is 13.70%. That doesn't mean every year produces this same return. That time period includes 91 individual one-year returns. These returns ranged from a gain of 53.99% (in 1933) to a loss of 43.34% (in 1931). Lest you think these wild swings are limited to the Depression era, the post-World War II data is just as volatile. The biggest gain was 52.62% (in 1954) and the largest loss was 37.00% (in 2008). That's a lot of uncertainty!

Let's see how time heals this "wound" of uncertainty. The time span from 1929 through 2017 contains 22 70-year periods. The median average annual 70-year return was 11.17% The best average annual 70-year return was a gain of 11.92% while the worst average annual 70-year return was a gain of 10.40%. That's a spread of only 1.52% among all the 70-year returns versus a spread of 97.35% for the one-year data. See how time (the professionals call it "time diversification") reduces uncertainty?

In fact, the graph on the next page represents the highest, median, and lowest average annual return for rolling time periods from 1926 through 2016. It clearly shows a reduction in the uncertainty of annual returns as you extend the time span from years to decades.

This graph also shows us something else, and it's rather interesting. The average median return for all the rolling periods is 11.03%. Look at the solid line on the graph. This represents the median average annual return for each rolling time period. See how remarkably flat it is?

Now, truth be told, we can't use past market performance to predict future market performance. Why? Because the future is uncertain. That being said, the future has always been uncertain, and yet, we witnessed an average annual return on U.S. stocks of 11% from 1926 through 2016. A lot of bad stuff happened during those ninety-one years. We've had multiple severe recessions, a Great Depression, a World War, a Cold War (and countless other wars), hurricanes, earthquakes, and any number of natural and man-made disasters. Do you think people didn't live in uncertainty back in the day? Your reaction might mimic my "in-hindsight-business-template" feeling, but, and you can ask anyone old enough to remember living through these events, there were definitely times when people wondered if there would even be a tomorrow.

Average Annual Returns for Rolling Time Periods (U.S. Stocks – 1926-2016)

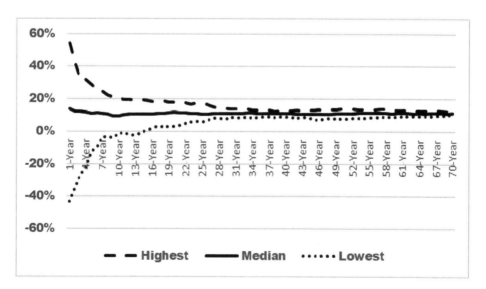

What will the world be like in 70 years when today's newborn babies retire? Who knows? What will the market return over that time period? Who knows? Intuition suggests, however, that the world will be a better place and the average annual market return over that time period will be 11%. Intuition isn't much, but at least it gives us a basis for going forward.

You might therefore ask, "If the average annual return is 11% of the 70 years a Child IRA exists before the child retires, why don't we use that number rather than the 8% in our assumptions? Well, in a word, "uncertainty." Recall my answer to those who told me I wasn't afraid of risk. I'm risk-averse. My figuring is this: Between inflation, fees, and bad luck, that 3% haircut ought to account for most of the things likely to erode returns.

For the record, after contributing $1,000 a year from the moment a baby is born until that child reaches birthday number 19, the 8% annual return assumption used here produces a value of $2,267,361 by the time said baby (née "child," now adult) retires at age 70. If we used the median 70-year average annual return of 11.17%, that value at age 70 would be $14,279,700. Incidentally, this number ranges from $9,159,112 if you were unlucky enough to begin the Child IRA during the worst performing 70-year period (10.40%) to $21,967,967 if the stars aligned just right and you began your Child IRA during the best performing 70-year period (11.92%).

Before you get too excited about those eight-digit home-run numbers, keep in mind the raw average annual return numbers probably include some factor for inflation. That's because stocks are generally considered a hedge against inflation. In order words, stock prices tend to go up as inflation goes up. Another way to think of this is, seventy years from now, $10 million might be only worth what $2 million is worth today. So, those home-runs might need to have an asterisk by them since they have been juiced up by inflation.

But you can't hit the ball if you don't swing the bat. Before you start spending these imaginary millions, you need to get the ball rolling and establish that Child IRA for your child. The next chapter tells you something about the Child IRA you may not have realized. It's not a show-stopper, but neither is it the IRA you're used to.

CHAPTER SIXTEEN:
NOT YOUR FATHER'S IRA – HOW TO OPEN A NEW CHILD IRA FOR YOUR CHILD OR GRANDCHILD

If you're like most Americans who have IRAs, you're familiar with how easy it is to set them up. Simply go to your friendly neighborhood bank, broker, or mutual fund, sign on the dotted line and – Bingo! – you're done and the IRA is ready to start accepting your annual contribution. The Child IRA, while still an IRA, isn't quite that easy. It's not hard, but it's not that easy. You caught a glimpse of this in Amy Bernstein's creation of IRAs for her children.

By the way, Amy referenced something she read in the 1990s about establishing IRAs for teenage children. Indeed, for many years the concept of a "child IRA" referred to either adult children saving for retirement or getting teenage children started on the road to retirement saving. The experience of the Bernstein family shows how this is done. It's possible the article that inspired her might have been found in "Kiplinger's 1999 Tax-Saving Guide." This was a special supplement to *USA Weekend* distributed to participating newspapers nationwide on Sunday, March 14, 1999. At its peak, Gannett's *USA Weekend* was the second largest Sunday magazine and distributed through more than 800 newspapers.[1]

Kiplinger's 1999 Tax Saving Guide contained the article "Make Your Child a Millionaire." The article begins "How would you like to teach yourself an invaluable, double-edged lesson about tax planning and long-term investing? Oh, and set them on the road to being millionaires at the same time?" It details how a 16-year old who sets up an IRA and then contributes $2,000 for just three consecutive years will end up with $1,111,000 when that teenager retires at age 67. Kiplinger's example assumes the 11% annual return based on the data we showed in the previous chapter.

The article was brief (about 600 words) and didn't go into much detail. Still, this idea of targeting teenager workers as potential IRA contributors has been a prominent marketing strategy of financial advisers for quite some time (and still is today). A typical example was this paragraph under the heading "When children enter the working world" from a column called "Financial Focus," written by two brokers in Carlinville, Illinois for their local paper:

"Encourage IRA contributions – An Individual Retirement Account (IRA) is a great retirement savings vehicle. As long as your children have earned income, they may contribute to an IRA, so you may want to help them max out on their contributions each year. While you can't directly contribute to a child's IRA, you can write a check to your child and encourage him or her to use it for funding an IRA."[2]

So, where do you go to set up a Child IRA? "Most companies don't have IRA fees anymore, so most major discount or online brokerage houses will do this," says Jenkin, co-CEO and Founder of oXYGen Financial in Alphareta, Georgia. It's likely they won't give you advice. So, you either go that route or you have an advisor who will include the account in the overall family accounts or do the work pro bono."

In January 2016, Fidelity introduced a specific program geared towards teenage IRAs. Called "Fidelity Roth IRA for Kids,"[3] the well-regarded mutual fund company made a concerted effort (and continues to do so) to educate families on the benefits of having their high school children establish IRAs. "When we launched the product, we did outreach and marketing online, in our branches, and direct mailing – emails and letters – to customers about the product," says Maura Cassidy, vice president of retirement, Fidelity. "Our representatives may also suggest the product to customers as they have planning sessions with those customers. We also try to get the word out via media outlets like yours that people should consider saving in a Roth for Kids."

Financial service firms often incorporate teenage IRA education into their standard IRA literacy materials as, while targeting different age groups, both use the same retirement saving vehicle – the IRA. Like any other IRA a Child IRA can only accept contributions based on the earned income of the owner (in this case, the child). Cassidy says that income "could be from a job at a family business or as a model/actor, as suggested; other jobs could be paid internships or summer jobs." These jobs can be as mundane as "babysitting or mowing lawns."[4]

This is what makes the Child IRA so rare, especially among younger children. "The child has to have income to be eligible for the account, plus the child would not need to spend this money, so it is not a common practice among your average family," says Christine Russell, Senior Manager, Retirement and Annuities at TD Ameritrade. "With that said, it is not unusual in the retirement industry, especially among children of the wealthy."

While the earned income requirement might seem an obvious obstacle, less apparent is the technical twist required when opening up an IRA for a minor child. "When an individual establishes an IRA, he or she is entering into a contract with the financial institution sponsoring the IRA," says Timothy Stokes, a spokesman for Vanguard. "Due to restrictions on the ability of a minor to enter into a valid contract, Vanguard IRA documentation must be signed by a custodian, who must also be listed on the account. IRAs for minors cannot be opened online. Once a minor reaches the age of maturity for their state of residence, he or she can request the 'A Minor' designation be removed."

According to Fidelity, "Minors cannot generally open brokerage accounts in their own name until they are 18, so a Roth IRA for Kids requires an adult to serve as custodian. The custodian maintains control of the child's Roth IRA, including decisions about contributions, investments, and distributions. In addition, statements are sent to the custodian. However, the minor remains the beneficial account owner and the funds in the account must be used for the benefit of the minor. When the minor reaches a certain required age, typically either 18 or 21 in most states, the assets must be transferred to a new account in his/her name. Once the minor reaches age 21, he/she can request a transfer of the assets to his/her own independently owned account."[5]

While opening a "Custodial" or "Minor" IRA sounds complicated, it's really no different that the custodial accounts parents have been setting up for their minor children for years. "We use TD Ameritrade as our custodian," says Marianela Collado, CEO and Senior Financial Advisor with Tobias Financial Advisors in Plantation, Florida. "I can't speak to any other custodian, but it would be important to work with an adviser who works with a custodian that offers a free trade platform so that the earnings don't get consumed with fees. That is super important."

"It is straightforward: An IRA application is completed and signed," says Russell. "Some IRA vendors will not accept minor IRAs as a business policy, but at TDAmeritrade we do and are happy to open the account. Requirements are: The minor IRA has one Account Owner (the minor) and one Custodian. The Custodian signs the application, oversees and operates the account, and must be the parent or legal guardian. Minors have to be below the age of majority for his/her state, not just below 18."

The Nuts and Bolts for Establishing a Child IRA: An Example

Anyone below the age of 18 must use a "Custodial" IRA. They cannot set their own IRA until their 18th birthday. This doesn't prevent them from establishing an IRA as a minor, they just need to have a custodian do it for them. Once a child reaches the age of maturity (between 18 and 21 depending on the state), the Custodial IRA must revert to the "child" (now adult) owner, and the custodian duties are formally terminated.

Things get a bit dicey with the age requirements. For example, if the child's birthday is on February 6th, and they want to establish an IRA the year they turn 18 for earnings they made the previous year (when they were 17), there are two different scenarios. First, if the IRA is established before February 6th (i.e., before the child's 18th birthday), then it must be a Custodial IRA. Second, if the IRA is established on

February 6th or later (i.e., on or after the child's 18th birthday), then it must be a standard IRA.

This brings up an interesting question. What happens if a Custodial IRA is established when the child is, say, ten-years old. Now, the strange thing about this child is, although he lives in Denver, Colorado, he's a big Buffalo Bills fan. Actually, it's not so strange. His family moved to the Mile High City from Buffalo when he was in kindergarten. He celebrates his 18th birthday and is showered with Bills jerseys, caps, and a signed Doug Flutie poster (don't ask why). He's old enough now that he can (heaven forbid) immediately go on eBay and sell those items. Oddly, though, he can't assume the full rights to his Child IRA. Why? Because the age of maturity in Colorado is 21. That means he needs to wait another three years before he can transfer the IRA to his full ownership.

On the other hand, had his family never moved away from Buffalo, he would have had the opportunity to take full control of his IRA on his 18th birthday. The age of majority in New York, as it is in all but four other states (Alabama, Colorado, Mississippi, and Nebraska) at the time of this writing, is 18 years.

Once it's determined the child has earned income, establishing an IRA for that child isn't too difficult.

Go into the office of your favorite financial services firm and ask for a "Custodial IRA Application" (it may also be called a "Minor Child IRA" or "IRA for a Minor Child" application). Bear in mind, some institutions do not provide for these types of IRAs, but most major banks, brokerage firms, and mutual fund companies do (you can access Fidelity's application on-line). There may be a minimum deposit required to open the account.

For example, a recent visit to the local Schwab office yielded a form called the "Schwab Custodial IRA Application." This four-page application appears very similar to a standard custodial account application. You'll need to complete information (including name, address and Social Security Number) for both the child as well as the custodian. Only the custodian is required to sign the application.

The first question many people ask is "Who should be the custodian of the Child IRA?" The custodian can be any adult, but it's most commonly the parent or grandparent. Aunts, Uncles, other members of the family, and even close family friends can also serve as custodians. It's a good idea to identify and indicate who the successor custodian will be in case the assigned custodian can no longer fulfill the duties.

Once the paperwork is completed, signed by the custodian, and handed to (in this case) Schwab along with Schwab's required minimum deposit of $100, the Child IRA (technically a "Custodial IRA") is open.

Ah, yes, as simple as pie, except for the fact we overlooked an important "first" decision. Before you set up the Child IRA, you need to decide whether it will be a Roth or a traditional IRA? Don't know the difference? Don't know the advantages and disadvantages of each? The answers lie ahead in the next chapter.

CHAPTER SEVENTEEN:
TO ROTH OR NOT TO ROTH?

Whether it's mowing the lawn or babysitting, minor children can place earned income into an IRA. The question is: Which one? The traditional or the Roth? For some of you, the better question is: What's the difference?

The traditional IRA was created under ERISA in 1974. It allowed you to make a $1,500 tax-deductible contribution to an Individual Retirement Account ("IRA") as a means of encouraging more people to save for their own retirement and rely less on corporate pension plans. The maximum contribution was raised to $2,000 in 1981. Since then the limit has gone up regularly to where it is today (2017) – $5,500 per person with an addition $1,000 "catch-up" allowance for people age 50 and older.

The traditional IRA, while offering a tax break at the beginning and permitting tax-free growth, contained one stipulation: when you withdraw money after age 59½, you had to finally pay taxes on it. After a couple of decades of this, people started to think it might make sense to add a "pay me now" alternative to this already existing "pay me later" option. To answer this need, in 1997 Congress created the Roth IRA.

The Roth IRA is treated exactly the same as a traditional IRA save for two very important differences. First, the bad news: There is no tax deduction associated with contributing to a Roth IRA. Second, we can't have bad news without some counterbalancing good news: You pay no taxes on any withdrawals (as long as you wait five years after contributing to the Roth before withdrawing).

"In terms of flexibility of withdrawals (i.e. availability to pull from the account before age 59½ without penalty) the Roth IRA will give the owner the ability to withdraw the contributions to the account on a tax-free and penalty-free basis after the contribution has been in the account for at least 5 years," says Alex Vaccarella, a financial planner at AEPG Wealth Strategies in Warren, New Jersey. "There are no exemptions for the investment growth on those contributions, however. As an example, if I am working and manage to put away $10k into my Roth over two years (say, $5k at age 15, $5k at age 16) I will be able to withdraw $5k tax and penalty free from the account when I turn 20, and by the time I am 21 I will be able to pull the full $10k in contributions. Assuming I earned 5% per year on that money, my account balance should be in excess of $13k when I turn 21, so I'll be left with $3k+ in the Roth after I pull my $10k in contributions."

The basic difference, then, between a traditional IRA and a Roth IRA is this: A traditional IRA is a tax-deferred (i.e., "pay me later") retirement savings vehicle while a Roth IRA is an after-tax (i.e., "pay me now") retirement savings vehicle. The differences can be important considerations when determined which flavor of IRA to choose when opening a Child IRA.

So, what are the most important factors parents need to consider? Financial planner Charles C. Scott, founder of Pelleton Capital Management and co-creator of FinancialChoicesMatter.com in Scottsdale, Arizona, says, "The key is whether a tax deduction matters or not. The traditional IRA is deductible, the Roth IRA is not.

Clearly, the specifics of one's tax situation represents the highest priority item when deciding whether to open a traditional IRA or a Roth IRA. "The biggest difference is the taxation," says Derek Hagen, Founder of Fireside Financial LLC in Minneapolis, Minnesota. "Deposits into a traditional IRA are made pretax (meaning you get a deduction on your current year's taxes), but then you have to pay tax on the withdrawals. Deposits into a Roth IRA are made after tax (meaning you do not get a deduction), but you don't have to pay taxes on the withdrawals. So, the difference really comes down to whether you think you will have a lower tax rate now or in the future."

Think about this for a moment. It is the child who must earn the money that is placed into the Child IRA. Is it likely the child will earn as much as an adult? "The most significant difference between traditional and Roth IRAs is when the saver will be taxed," says Jason J. Howell, President of Jason Howell Company in Vienna, Virginia. "High income earners, unlike a child, can benefit from a tax break today. Typically, someone who intends to make more money later in life may benefit from paying taxes today (and not tomorrow)."

While how and when taxes are applied may be the first main difference between the Roth and the traditional IRA, there is another difference. "The second main difference is when the money can be withdrawn," says Zach Stuppy, President of Brave Boat Capital Advisors located in Boston, Massachusetts. "For basic distributions, the distribution age is 59½ for both IRA types. However, the Roth IRA offers some flexibility for early withdrawal. You can take penalty free, early withdrawals from a Roth to pay for education expenses or for a first-time home purchase (with limitations). A Roth also allows for the return of principal without penalty."

It's not just "when" you can take the money out, it's also when you "must" take the money out. "The traditional IRA grows tax deferred but you pay tax when the money is withdrawn in 50+ years," says Michael Landsberg, a Partner at Landsberg Bennett Private Wealth Management in Punta Gorda, Florida. Unlike the traditional IRA, which requires distributions to begin no later than age 70½, Landsberg points out "the Roth grows tax free and there is no tax or mandatory distribution at age 70½."

With these factors in mind, is one type of IRA better than the other when it comes to establishing a Child IRA? Financial advisers from across the nation are generally of one mind on this. "Unless the child's income puts them into 25% or more marginal tax bracket, ROTH! ROTH! ROTH!" says Ilene Davis. "Why give up potential tax free future income to get a 10-15% tax deduction. If the child does a good job saving through life, tax bracket in retirement should be higher."

It's a straight forward calculation. "With minor children, under normal circumstances, I think it is always better to use a Roth IRA," says Vern Sumnicht, CEO/Founder of iSectors® LLC & Sumnicht & Associates LL in Appleton, Wisconsin. "As long as the minor has earned income, up to $5,500 a year can be contributed to a Roth IRA. Those dollars will grow tax free for the minor child for a long time."

The "pay me now" appeal of the Roth is quite apparent given the tax circumstances of most children. "The Roth IRA is hands down the better choice in this situation," says Scott Vance, Enrolled Agent at Taxvanta in Cary, North Carolina. "The Roth is contributed after-tax, but is not taxed when taken out. A traditional IRA is a tax deduction when a contribution is made but upon withdrawal it is taxed as ordinary income. So, in the case of a child, using a traditional would provide rather small deductions since generally when children are minors their income level is low as is their tax rate. The Roth would not provide that rather small deduction now but many years down the road in Retirement the Roth would be withdrawn tax free, during a period when the tax rates are projected to be higher thereby providing a much better overall deal."

Simply stated, the tax-deferred advantage of the traditional IRA does not exist for most children. Ken Hoyt, of Hoyt Wealth Management in Westford, Massachusetts, says, "When it comes to minor children, the Roth IRA wins out every time. Here's why: Roth IRAs offer no immediate tax benefit, but they grow completely tax-free if withdrawn after age 59½. Minor children typically are in the lowest possible tax bracket, or pay no taxes at all; however, they will always assuredly be in a higher tax bracket later in life. Conversely, a traditional IRA offers an immediate tax benefit which the minor child will not realize."

"Minor children don't need the deduction, so the Roth will always be the better choice," says Scott. "Having to pay income tax on a small amount of money today and not ever having to pay it again makes way more sense. Roths grow tax-free and the money comes out tax-free. There are some rules for the Roth that limit the tax-free withdrawal feature, namely that a Roth account (not all Roth accounts) needs to be open for a minimum of 5 years, after which the contributions can be taken out without tax. Also, the tax-free feature on the growth inside the Roth only happens after the owner is 59½ or older. These are 'retirement' accounts after all."

With a Roth IRA, it's very possible a child will never pay taxes on earnings and the growth of those earnings. "A Roth IRA is better in almost all instances," says Stuppy. "The minor is contributing after tax dollars to the IRA and with most minors earning so little they would be in a very low tax bracket or pay 0%. Therefore, no taxes would be owed up front and any distributions would be tax-free. This leads to a situation where the minor could potentially never pay taxes on these assets. The withdrawal flexibility a Roth IRA offers also makes it a better choice in almost all scenarios. This flexibility allows the money to be withdrawn early for a number of reasons and thus it isn't tied up until the minor turns 59½."

Because the child's tax bracket is usually very low, it even makes sense to pay those small taxes now in exchange for avoiding higher taxes in the future. "In general, we recommend using the Roth IRA," says Ben Westerman, Senior Vice President at HM Capital Management in St. Louis, Missouri. "Even if the parent ends up paying a little bit of the child's tax (via the "kiddie tax"), as long as the parent can afford and wants to pay the tax, the Roth IRA is the way to go."

Hagen agrees. He says, "A Roth is best when you are currently in a low tax bracket. Pay the tax when the rates are lowest. By using this for children with earned income, they will never have to pay taxes on the account again (as long as they hold the account for at least 5 years before withdrawing)."

Is there ever a time when it might make sense to use a traditional IRA as the preferred vehicle for a Child IRA? Yes, but those times are very rare and very narrowly defined. "There are very few instances when a traditional IRA makes sense for a minor," says Stuppy. "Most minors make such little money that they will owe no or very minimal taxes so the upfront tax savings of a traditional IRA would be negligible. The only instance that it may make sense is if the minor makes a high level of earnings. In this case, the traditional IRA would help to offset the tax burden."

Still, there may be advantages to showing no after-tax income, regardless of how small it is. "I guess the only area where a traditional IRA would make sense for a child would be in the case of a child who earns a lot of money and is in need of ways to reduce their AGI to become eligible for some credits or deductions," says Vance.

Besides a large income and qualifying for other benefits (like college financial aid), traditional IRAs do offer additional perks not found in a Roth IRA. Landsberg says, "There are also some extra abilities inside the traditional IRA to withdraw for college or a first home that the Roth does not have."

The decision may seem cut and dried, but it's always best to consult with the appropriate advisor to make sure the appropriate type of IRA is used when establishing a Child IRA. "The traditional vs Roth IRA debate is not a new one, and there are valid arguments on both sides," says Hoyt. "Traditional IRAs are clearly better when the account owner is currently in a high tax bracket but expects to be in a lower bracket when retired. The opposite is true for Roth IRAs. If someone's future tax bracket is unclear, then there is no clear advantage to either type of IRA."

There is one disadvantage a Roth IRA has compared to a traditional IRA. With a Roth IRA, you can withdraw your original contribution after five years. You don't need a reason. You can use it for anything. It can provide the necessary funds for a down payment on a house. It can help pay for a college education – even graduate school! Of course, if you don't need a reason, that means you can withdraw the funds for less noble reasons, like buying that 80" 3-D Smart TV, purchasing not just a Mustang, but a Shelby GT350®, or ordering a, well, you get the drift. The point is, unlike the safeguards imposed by the withdrawal restrictions of a traditional IRA, the Roth IRA requires steadfast discipline to avoid the temptation of premature withdrawal.

You're probably thinking, "But I thought early withdrawal was an advantage to the Roth?" It is, but only in the sense that there's an emergency and there is no other alternative. The problem is, once you withdraw, you lose all the advantages of 70 years of uninterrupted compound growth. That might be too big a price to pay for the immediate gratification of going from zero-to-60 in 4.3 seconds behind the 526 horsepower 5.2L Ti-VCT V-8 engine.

In either case, go ahead and make your decision. Then, let the contributions begin!

Oh. Wait. The child has to earn that income first. Well, as we said, that's the real hurdle in this entire enterprise. Russell says there are several typical earnings opportunities for children. She cites "family businesses (where the child is paid a wage), and child models/actors. Perhaps another group might be younger professional athletes with high income from endorsements (Olympians for example). Advisors and those in the financial services industry also open these accounts for their own children who have income, to start the children on a long-term savings path."

Alas, child labor is a complicated matter. But there are loopholes, as the next chapter reveals.

Chapter Eighteen:
Child Labor – The Pregnant Pause

It was over in less than half an hour, but, for many, it was just ten minutes that separated them from life and death.[1] Esther Harris was moments away from clocking out of her bookkeeping job on that tragic day of Saturday, March 25, 1911. The company she worked for occupied the top three floors of the a ten-floor building at the corner of Greene Street and Washington Place in New York City. At 4:40pm, a mere five minutes before quitting time,[2] someone threw a cigarette in a scrap heap under a cutting table.[3] Within seconds that flicker of flame became an inferno that engulfed the 4,500 square feet on the eighth floor before quickly spreading to the upper two floors.

With no means of escape, Esther was pushed by the hundreds of workers to the nearest elevator shaft. She jumped through the open door and grabbed the cable. She shimmied down to the fifth floor before her strength failed her. Her hands slipped from the cable and Esther plunged fifty feet down the shaft to certain death. Only death did not come quickly. Esther's limp body was removed from the lifeless bodies of the victims that fell before her, and she was quickly taken to St. Vincent Hospital. There, looking over the still figure of the young woman, a nurse asked the doctor "What should be done with her?"[4]

"Leave her alone, as she only has a few minutes to live," were the last words Esther heard before her world went dark.[5]

Of the 146 victims from the infamous Triangle Shirt Waist Factory fire, the youngest were 14-year-olds Kate Leone and "Sara" Rosaria Maltese.[6] This tragedy led to many workplace laws. You might even think the death of these two 14-year-olds would have inspired more strict child labor laws. It did not.

"Unlike the Triangle Shirtwaist Factory Fire, which led directly to workplace safety laws, there was no single person or event that directly caused child labor laws to happen," says Michael Cardman, Legal Editor at XpertHR in New Providence, New Jersey. "Rather, protecting children from unsafe working conditions was one of the many goals of the broader Progressive Movement of the late 19th and early 20th centuries. As a result of the Progressive Movement, child labor laws were passed by the US Congress in the early 20th Century. But these laws were declared unconstitutional by the US Supreme Court. It wasn't until the Great Depression struck that we got the main child labor law we know today. Child labor restrictions were included in the Fair Labor Standards Act (FLSA) in 1938. One of the central pieces of legislation in FDR's New Deal, the FLSA is widely credited with helping to spur employment and improve working conditions for minors. Also, all 50 states and the District of Columbia passed similar child labor laws in the wake of the FLSA."

On the face of it, at the federal level child labor laws appear quite restrictive. "In general, a child is not allowed to work until the age of 14," says Vance. "From the ages of 14 until 16 children are limited in the amount of hours they can work. In general, any child under the age of 18 cannot work in any job that is deemed 'Hazardous.' The US Department of Labor provides these general guidelines, and states implement their own state specific child work limitations within these general guidelines. The Department of Labor also provides for exceptions. A commonly used one is that most of the rules do not apply to a minor child working in a family owned business."

State laws can be even more restrictive. "The California Labor Code protects any workers under the age of 18, and has additional rules for when and how many hours they can work," says Evelyn Cook, President of Cook CPA Group in Roseville, California. "Children aged six through 15 need to attend school full-time unless they already graduated early or fulfill other requirements. Most states allow 16-year-olds to work, and they may be able to school part-time."

If children under the age of 14 can't work, what about all those famous child actors we keep reading about? Do they work for free? Have they discovered a way to circumvent child labor laws? "These children do not skirt the law," says Cardman. "Rather, there is a specific exemption from the FLSA's child labor provisions for 'any child employed as an actor or performer in motion pictures or theatrical productions, or in radio or television productions.'"

Ryan Neumeyer, an attorney at McDonald Hopkins, LLC in Cleveland, Ohio, says, "29 U.S.C. 213(c) provides an exemption from the child labor provisions for 'any child employed as an actor or performer in motion pictures or theatrical productions, or in radio or television productions.' Many states also have rules dealing with minor performers." We'll get to some of those special state rules in a moment.

Child labor laws weren't designed to act as an insurmountable obstacle. Instead, they offer guidelines for what needs to be done in order to allow a child to get paid for work. Getting a child to earn income isn't normally something a child can do alone. It often requires parental consent. Technically, even something as routine and commonplace as babysitting or mowing the lawn needs to first be cleared with the child's parents. Matt C. Pinsker, a law professor at Virginia Commonwealth University in Henrico, Virginia, says, "Child labor laws are premised on the legal principle that children are unable to consent. The incapacity of a child to give consent applies to labor, contracts, sex, medical procedures, etc. When children do find employment, such as child actors, their parents or guardians give consent on their behalf." (See Chapter 23: "For Parents and Grandparents" for greater details on how child labor laws may apply to your specific circumstances.)

Here's a critically important loophole to child labor laws for parents interested in starting a Child IRA for their children: Family businesses are, for the most part, exempt from child labor laws. "Minors employed by a parent or guardian are exempt from the FLSA's minimum age requirements," says Cardman. "However, such family members are still prohibited from working in hazardous occupations like mining, logging, manufacturing, etc."

Since parents face fewer restrictions when hiring their own minor children, the next question might be "At what age does it make sense for a child to begin working?" "In most cases a parent can hire a child to work in the family business as long as the working hours do not exceed certain limits and the tasks are not considered dangerous," says Steven J. Weil, President of RMSAccounting in Fort Lauderdale, Florida. "At what age a child can work depends on the age they are capable of performing a task that has business value. The wages also need to be in line with the task performed. Take, for example, the person who has a children's store and needs models for use in car seat or other promotions. So long as the amount paid to the child is in line with what one would pay any other child model, there is no problem. As a child gets older they could be paid to tag merchandise, sweep up, put merchandise back on the shelves, etc. It all depends on their ability at each age. A teenager could learn to answer phones, make copies or do office work. The key is the ability to do meaningful work that if not done by the child would have to be done by others. We have seen infant models, teenage bookkeepers, even young web designers and much more over the years. Teaching your child, no matter how young, to perform useful work that has value and paying for it, is a great lesson that will serve them well later in life."

Many parents who operate family owned businesses employ their children for reasons that may benefit the parents' tax circumstances, too. "Generally, you are exempt from child labor laws with respect to your own children," says Tom Wheelwright, CPA, founder of ProVision CPAs and author of Tax-Free Wealth. "Small children can do a lot of things, such as modeling for the family business, bookkeeping, office work, and clean up. There are terrific tax benefits to hiring your children. First, you move money from your tax bracket into their tax bracket. Earned income is not subject to the kiddie tax (where investment income of a child is taxed at their parents' tax rate). Second, if you pay them from a sole proprietorship or partnership that only you and/or your spouse owns, then there is no Social Security tax for children under the age of 18."

You might be familiar with what happens to your paycheck between the time your employer issues it and the time you deposit it in your account. The government takes out its cut of the pie. Among the largest chunks of these payroll taxes is the Federal Insurance Contributions Act (FICA) tax. "Every worker must pay FICA taxes," says Cook. "If you are an employee, your employer will withhold your FICA taxes and cover their share. If you are self-employed as a sole proprietor or an independent contractor, your FICA taxes are covered by your self-employment (SECA) taxes. However, self-employed people may get a tax deduction for paying these taxes."

It's a rite of passage for young workers that happens every time they open up their first paycheck. How many parents get a chuckle when their working children get their first paystub only to find they only get to spend their net pay, not what they thought they were earning (i.e., their gross pay). "As an employer paying wages there is a requirement to hold FICA tax on all employees and therefore there could not be an exception for a minor," says Suzanne Weathers, Owner at Weathers & Associates Consulting in Spokane, Washington. "In theory being a contractor would be an option BUT the tax code defines who is an employee as 'if the employer can control what will be done and how it will be done.'"

A child could be an independent contractor, but there are greater tax savings when the child works for the parents' firm. Weil says, "If a child is under 18 and is an employee of a parents' sole proprietorship, they do not have to pay into the FICA system."

"There is a potential way for a minor to avoid FICA taxes" says Joshua Wu, a tax attorney at JW Law PLLC in Washington, DC with experience helping individuals and small businesses comply with federal tax laws. "Payments to a child under age 18 who works for his or her parent in a trade or business are not subject to social security and Medicare taxes (FICA) if the trade or business is a sole proprietorship or a partnership in which each partner is a parent of the child. Payments to a child under age 21 who works for his or her parent in a trade or business are not subject to Federal Unemployment Tax Act (FUTA) tax."

Let's sum this up. First, children under 18 don't have to pay FICA or FUTA payroll taxes when working for their parents in businesses organized as sole proprietorships or partnerships. Second, a Roth IRA grows tax-free and its withdrawals are tax-free. This means, if parents operating a sole proprietorship or partnership employ their newborn for $1,000 a year until that newborn turns 19 and puts that annual earnings into a Child IRA, that newborn will have access to $2.25 million at age 70, AND THAT ENTIRE AMOUNT WILL BE EARNED WITHOUT EVER PAYING TAXES!

"Impossible!" you might say. But, you know, that's the same thing the doctors said about Esther Harris when they brought her to St. Vincent's Hospital following the Triangle Shirt Waist fire. She was paralyzed and not expected to ever recover. Yet, on April 7, 1913, more than two years after that tragic fire, doctors pronounced Harris was able to walk and completely cured.[7]

In the Depression Era, child labor laws were enacted to prevent the abuse often seen in the hiring of children. While those laws make it nearly impossible for children below the age of 16 to obtain gainful employment, there are opportunities for even pre-teens to earn a paycheck, including some many parents have overlooked. What are these opportunities, and what exactly is considered "income"? Turn the page and discover the answers.

CHAPTER NINETEEN:
JOBS FOR YOUNGSTERS

Much of what's written in the media focuses on convincing adults to save for their own retirement. In establishing Child IRAs for them, we can teach kids at a younger age the importance of saving for retirement. Is there a chance that, by doing this, they'll need less convincing to save for retirement when they're adults? The only way we'll find the answer to this question is if parents begin opening these long-term investment accounts for their children.

"I can speak to this one from personal experience," says Paul R. Ruedi, a Financial Advisor at Ruedi Wealth Management in Champaign, Illinois. "The best way to emphasize the importance of saving and investing for retirement to children is to set up investment accounts for them when they are young, designate the funds in it as their money so they take an interest, and let them watch it grow over time. This is exactly what my grandparents did for all their other grandchildren when I was in grade school – they opened brokerage accounts for us and let us choose a handful of stocks to invest in. I am now 28 and have seen that money grow for almost two decades. Nothing can convince you of the power of investing more effectively than watching your own money grow over a long time horizon. I am extremely thankful to my grandparents for this lesson."

Ruedi had the advantage of opening up taxable accounts, not a Child IRA. Like any other IRA, a Child IRA requires children to earn income. This income can come from anywhere. "The IRS defines income as 'all income from whatever source derived'," says Evelyn Cook. "This even includes cash for babysitting or mowing a neighbor's lawn, and any 'under-the-table' payments technically need to be reported as income if you make enough money throughout the year."

Once a child earns income, then the operative question is how it should be reflected on annual income tax filings and on whose filing it should be reflected. "Anyone who makes income must file taxes, including your children," says Cook. "However, if they are young enough, you may file taxes for them. This includes federal, state, and local taxes – but deductions and limits might mean your child does not need to file."

The exact status and process involved in filing the forms can be a tad complicated in some circumstances. For that reason, it's always best to consult a professional tax advisor to know what's best for you and your child. "There are numerous issues with respect to minor children who earn income from their work," says Joshua Wu. "While different states have age limits on when children can work, the IRS considers all income, from whatever source derived, to be subject to taxation. Income from the work of a minor child is generally reported on the child's federal income tax return. However, a parent of a child under age 19 (or under age 24 if a full-time student) may be able to elect to include the child's interest and dividend income (but not earned income from work) on the parent's return. Otherwise, a minor is considered a separate taxpayer and must file a return. If the child is unable to file a return because of age or for any other reason, the partner or guardian is responsible for filing the return."

Sometimes the decision on who should file can be triggered by earned income thresholds. "The child does not have to file a separate tax return unless they have earned income of over $6,300 (2016's figure) for the year," says Vance. "If the child has unearned income (i.e., interest, dividends or capital gains), the child will have to file a separate return if the total amount of unearned income is greater than $1,050 in the year. The bigger question is does it make sense to include the child's income in the parents return or let them file on their own? Generally, if the child files a return, they will be able to recover withheld income taxes, the parent can still claim the dependency exemption for them. Also, adding a child's income into the parent's income could push the parent into a situation where they lose eligibility for certain credits or deductions."

Another reason to consult with an advisor might be due to certain minimum taxes parents could still be responsible for at either the state or federal level. Suzanne Weathers, says, "A child would report on their own return but could be taxed at their parents' rate if subject to the 'kiddie tax.' Teens typically earning less than the standard deduction will have no liability."

In addition to tax filing, several states require a certain percentage of a minor's earned income to be set aside in what's called a "Coogan Trust." Jackie Coogan may be best remembered for his role as Uncle Fester in the 1960s TV series *The Addams Family*, however, he broke into Hollywood as a youngster. In 1921, at the age of seven, Coogan played the title role in Charlie Chaplin's classic film *The Kid*. His mother squandered all his earnings, which provided the impetus for the California State Legislature to pass a law protecting the assets of child actors. Since then, New York, Louisiana, and New Mexico have passed similar laws.

So-called "Coogan Accounts" are custodial accounts, similar to the way a parent would open a Child IRA. "We have many kids that are working and have IRA's or Coogan Accounts by the age of 10," says Michelle Lyons, Founder & CEO of The BESTalent Group in Century City, California. "It is mandated in the State of California that all minors in the entertainment industry have Coogan accounts that at least 15% of the income they earn is saved until they are 18 years of age."

Lyons says she trains actors, models, etc. for two hours a week as young as 3 years old and no maximum on age. She outlined what we typically see child actors and models do, based on their age:

0-3 years: "Not very many agencies represent infants and toddlers. The majority of the ones that do expect a child to be at least 6 months and/or able to sit up for print ads and possibly diaper or Gerber commercials. Soap operas tend to use newborns because someone is always having a baby, but there are few agencies that supply the newborns. Just like every age group, the younger you are the less competitive this industry is."

4-8 years: "Talented kids in this age range are prodigies, (e.g., Raven Simone, Tiger Woods, Dakota Fanning, Haley Joel Osment, etc). This is the best age range to really develop a child on a craft. Kids are like sponges at this age and the possibilities are growing tremendously from print and commercials to runway and theatrical. This age range is also the easiest to sign with an agent."

9-11 years: "Selena Gomez and several Disney stars have been discovered in this age range. In the world of acting this is a key age group because this is the age group where talented kids start to divide from the rest." Lyons says children under 12 can only work 4 hours in a day.

12-15 years: "This is the key age range in modeling. High fashion modeling starts at 15 years and after 15 modeling becomes drastically more competitive." She also says child actors and models who are under 16 can only work 6 hours in a day.

16-18 years: "This is the age range where a lot of kids have adult mindsets so the competition is fiercer; however, for singers, dancers, and triple threats this is a key age range. This is a great age to get discovered for singing/dancing or to position yourself for a great performing arts college like Juilliard, NYU, Yale Drama, CALArts, etc."

Of course, children can earn income through other jobs. Here is a breakdown by age group to give you a sense for what's possible:

Pre-K: At the very youngest of ages (think first year), the child is not capable of doing anything except for modeling. As Lyons says, most agencies require tots to be at least six months old. Still photographs used in advertising represents the easiest way to generate earned income for babies. These can be sold or they can be used in family businesses for advertising purposes. As a child approached Kindergarten, they can start getting paid for doing simple jobs in the home. Andi Wrenn, a financial counselor and marriage coach in Raleigh, NC, says, "Folding laundry and other household help/chores," while Rachel Gottlieb, a New York-based financial planner and SVP at UBS Wealth Management, suggests, "Small jobs around the house, such as making the bed and cleaning their bedroom."

Elementary School: At this age, children can take on more formidable tasks. These can be "more structured household chores, such as taking out the trash, washing the car and unloading the dishwasher," says Gottlieb. For the family business, this is the envelope-stuffing-and-stamping age.

Middle School: By the time children reach the sixth grade, they are more than capable of assuming greater responsibilities. This is the age range when many children have their first "real" (i.e., non-family) job. For example, Wrenn says these kinds of jobs can include a "paper route, babysitting, mowing, shoveling, some states allow employment at 14 for certain stores and activities."

High School: Finally old enough to overcome the child labor law impediments, teenagers can get "regular jobs," as Wrenn says. These are the kinds of jobs we normally associate with pre-college workers. "At this age children are likely able to get more traditional part-time jobs, such as working in a local shop or restaurant," says Gottlieb.

Remember, the goal is to generate only $1,000 of earned income per year from the moment a baby is born until that baby turns nineteen. Putting that $1,000 of earned income into a Child IRA for those nineteen years will yield a windfall of $2.25 million when the child retires at age 70.

But, what happens if you've missed the Child IRA train? What if you're reading this book and you're saying to yourself, "But my child is already in kindergarten (or middle school, or high school, or college). Is it too late for me to start a Child IRA for them?" The quick answer is "No!" For the more detailed answer, turn to the next chapter.

CHAPTER TWENTY:
WHAT TO DO IF YOU MISSED
THE CHILD IRA TRAIN

June is the season of graduation parties. Whether newly minted from high school or college, these young minds leave the classroom full of vigor, ambition, and missing the one thing that's most important to them. Yes, we teach them to look to the next level quite well. We sate them with so much self-esteem they come brimming with confidence and high expectations. They're ready and willing to tackle new jobs, higher education, and a world they've been told is waiting for them with open arms.

Alas, amidst this unbridled enthusiasm sits an easily attainable goal all alone in a dimly lit corner. Aside from cobwebs and dust, its only covering is a faded sticky note with the words "open later – we have time" scrawled in child-like cursive on it. This is the goal we like to call "comfortable retirement."

We humans are a resilient species. We can accomplish almost anything given enough time, resources, and hard work. Unfortunately, we are also a species that enjoys to eat, to drink, and to be merry. We often put off to tomorrow things that we can (and should) do today. We quickly learn to prioritize goals not by some overarching strategy, but by the tick-tock of impending deadlines.

Of all the gifts we can offer graduates, even we miss the opportunity to help them focus on that which endures for a lifetime. We give cars (sometime, although rarely, a Shelby GT350® capable of going from zero-to-60 in 4.3 seconds behind the 526 horsepower 5.2L Ti-VCT V-8 engine), but, thanks to Henry Ford's brilliant innovation (not the automobile itself, but the concept of planned obsolescence), they last but a handful of years. We can give a wad of cash, but chances are that will end up merely buying the aforementioned car, and we end up with the same rusting result. We can give a good and meaningful book, but unless it can be read on the tiny screen, its greatest purpose will be to serve as a foundation to prop up some cheap furniture.

Enterprising parents and family members are now beginning to feel the best gift is to help reduce the graduate's loan burden. While that may be both helpful and practical, there is a greater gift, one more practical, one immensely helpful. This is the gift of The Child IRA, (although, at this point the "child" refers to the relationship and not the age, since college graduates tend to be adults).

Technically, you can't "give" an IRA. You can, however, give the cash necessary to start an IRA. Actually, the better way to do it is to bring the paperwork to the graduate so that you can be there when it's signed, then take it back and deposit your cash gift right into the new IRA account. By the time one graduates, one usually has (or will soon have) enough earned income to cover the maximum allowable annual IRA contribution (currently $5,500).

Let's say you're reading this book and you have come to the realization that you may have missed the train on this whole "Child IRA" thing. It's not too late to catch up. I can ask you to go back to Chapter 11 and take another look at Chart I. "Catching Up to the Child IRA," but you'll end up thumbing through the pages of this book and then lose your place. Besides, the print on that chart is probably too small for many to read. Instead, I'll do you a favor and tell you the key takeaway from that chart right here on this page.

It is possible to make amends for not reading this book a decade or so before it was written. No, you don't need a time machine to accomplish this, you just need the proper instructions. Fortune is with you today as I'm going to give those instructions to you right now:

1) Remember that graduation gift of an IRA you decided to give? Well, you need to offer to give this gift not just for graduation, but the several years after graduation.

2) Your (now adult) child will need to earn at least $5,500 during the year of graduation. For the purposes of this set of instructions, we'll assume your child graduates at age 22.

3) You bring your child the IRA paperwork, show them how to fill it out and where to sign. You may need to do this in the presence of the financial institution you will use to open the account. N.B.: Unlike the Custodial IRA that you must use for a minor child, this is a regular IRA since your child is now an adult.

4) You write a check for $5,500 and deposit it into the child's account.

5) Continue to gift your child $5,500 every year until your child's 40th birthday. That year you only need to gift $2,881 for depositing in the IRA.

6) Do nothing and earn an average of 8% a year (remember, that's 3% below the average annual return for US equities).

7) When the child retires at age 70, that IRA will have grown to $2.25 million!

I know, I know, not every child is on the same "age" calendar when it comes to graduating from college. Some try to save money and graduate a year early while others may take some time off and graduate a year later. All that changes is step 5) of the instructions. Here's how that step would read for someone graduating a year early and someone graduating a year later:

When a child graduates from college a year early (age 21):

5) Continue to gift your child $5,500 every year until your child's 36th birthday. That year you only need to gift $4,345 for depositing in the IRA.

When a child graduates from college a year later (age 23):

5) Continue to gift your child $5,500 every year until your child's 45th birthday. That year you only need to gift $1,679 for depositing in the IRA.

You might notice you don't have to give as much if you start earlier. In fact, when a child graduates at the usual age (22), parents will need to gift a total of $101,881 over 19 years to catch up to the original Child IRA. If a child graduates a year early, those gifts total only $86,845 over 16 years to catch up to the original Child IRA. When a child graduates a year later, to catch up to the original Child IRA parents must gift a total of $122,679 over a 23-year period. (Well, heck, you can't take it with you so what better way to spend it!)

If you're like many people, you're looking at these total numbers and thinking, "That's more than I earn!" Well, rest easy. The beauty of the gifting concept is that it doesn't have to come from one source. The parents don't have to foot the whole bill (or even any of it). The grandparents, aunts, uncles, and perhaps a friendly neighbor or two – anybody – can provide the money that will be contributed into the IRA. There are no tax implications for these gifts because the IRS allows you to give up to $10,000 per year to individuals, and the maximum contribution of $5,500 is well below that.

Offering an ongoing graduation gift of a Child IRA helps the graduate develop a habit for retirement saving. When that graduate retires at age 70, those little annual IRA contributions will have grown to more than $2.25 million dollars (that's assuming an annual return of 8%). Not too bad and way better than some car (even a Shelby GT350®).

Now, if you are in a position to hire an outside contractor, whether in your own business or as an employee of a business, there's something else you can do. Something more powerful than a mere Child IRA. In fact, think of it as a Child IRA on steroids. Of course, since we're talking only of IRAs, it's really not the focus of this book. Still, I'm not good at keeping secrets, so you can take a peek at Appendix IV to discover what this is. But you didn't hear it from me.

Are you ready to start a Child IRA? The next section provides the roadmap, no matter where you're starting.

SECTION FIVE:

– THE CHILD IRA FUTURE –

YOUR NEXT STEP

CHAPTER TWENTY-ONE:
GAMING AND SAVING

Long before he was married, Rodney Davis, a systems analyst, knew what his financial priorities were. Making good money and without the financial burden of having a family, the twenty-something year old did something rarely found in that age group: He focused squarely on what he wanted, made a plan on how to get there, then carried out that plan. As with many of his generation, the foundation of that plan would have made Lucy Van Pelt (of Charlie Brown fame) proud: Real estate.

Not only did Rodney buy his family home before he had a family (indeed, before he was married), he also invested in rental properties used by full-time students at a popular state university.

Well, time went on as it tends to do. Rodney married Erica, (by coincidence, also a systems analyst), and they had three wonderful sons, Alex, Ray, and Adam. Rodney and Erica continued to work hard at their jobs. Still, they had time for their boys, activities, from sports, to scouts, to robotics. The little side business of student rental property continued, too. When the boys got old enough, like all children whose family have their own business, it was the kids turn to toil the earth (or, in this case, wax the floors).

For Rodney, bringing the kids in to work and starting their Child IRAs went hand-in-hand. "There is an old wise tale that you have to hear about something ten times before you realize that you have heard it," says Rodney. "I had read and investigated opening up a Roth IRA for my wife and myself. Unfortunately, the limitations on how much you could invest into the Roth IRA reduced the amount that we could earn. That small return wasn't enough to excite either Erica or myself to open an account."

Then, one day, came the proverbial bolt from the blue. "While glancing through the *Bottom Line* publication, I read an article about setting up Roth IRAs for your children," recalls Rodney. "The article spoke about investing $4,000 a year for 10 years (age 15-25) and along with a conservative rate of return, your children would have hundreds of thousands of dollars at retirement age. The amount would even double or triple, if your children continued to invest after age 25. The concept hit me like a bolt of lightning, especially since the oldest of my rug rats had reached 15 years of age and all my kids were helping me with property maintenance on our rental properties."

Very quickly, as you might expect from a man of action, Rodney began moving his kids – one at a time – into Roth IRAs. "I started my two oldest kids (Alex and Ray) on their Roth IRA when they were 15 years old," says Rodney. "It was a perfect combination of teaching them the value of hard work, learning a skill, and investing for the future. Surprisingly, my kids did not see the opportunity that I saw in this endeavor. They focused on the hard work part of the job: cleaning apartments, landscaping yards, and painting rooms."

Perhaps now might be a useful time to digress with a funny story that many parents whose children help them in their business might recognize as typical with their kids, too. Rodney tells the tale like this:

"My youngest child, Adam, a teenager at the time, has a story which epitomizes the hardship of hard work. Alex, my oldest son, and I had sanded down the wood floors in an apartment to prepare for a coat of polyurethane. The plan was for Alex and I to polyurethane the edges of the rooms & hallway while Adam would then spread the polyurethane across the wide-open spaces, a relatively safe and harmless job with little room of getting it wrong. That was the plan, but we all know how plans go."

"My initial mistake was not introducing Adam to polyurethane first. I had popped open a can of polyurethane and began to set up Alex to start coating the edges. Adam decided to get up close and personal with the gallon can of polyurethane. The polyurethane fumes and strong odor caused him to repulse immediately, he ran out of the apartment while screaming, 'I'm not going near that stuff.' It took me over a half hour to convince him to come back in and try."

"When we went back into the apartment, he was not ready to polyurethane the floors. I realized that he needed more time to acclimate to the task at hand. While his big brother and I started the edge work, I had him stand behind us and watch. After about a half hour, he was ready to try and coat the floor of the room."

"I took some time to show him how to apply the polyurethane with long, even brush strokes. You know, the kind of things dads all over teach their kids. He's a fast learner and quickly took to the job. Meanwhile, Alex and I were way behind schedule and we needed to focus on completing the edge work."

"Now this is where the fun begins. Alex and I had completed the edge work in that room, so we moved on to the next room. Adam kept varnishing away, integrating his brush strokes with our edging. Little did we realize that instead of going across the room with his polyurethaning, he was going around the room in a clockwise fashion."

"A few minutes later we heard a yell from the other room, and, sure enough, he had painted himself into a circle in the middle of the room."

"Now, keep in mind, Adam is the most daring in the family. He was going to show us that he could jump from the center of the room to the doorway entrance. I had my doubts, but I didn't have a better idea at the time. He crouched down, like a tiger ready to leap upon its prey. He took one little step forwards and tried to leap. His front foot slid out from underneath him and he ended up on his butt on the newly covered polyurethane floor. To make it more of a catastrophe, he then flipped over onto his hands and feet to get off the floor. He was covered with sticky polyurethane from hands to toes."

"Needless to say, Adam did not care about his financial reward in spending money or in a Roth IRA that day."

Now that you've had your little chuckle at Adam's expense (in real life, he laughed, too), let's get back to the real story. The process of opening the Roth IRAs was a piece of cake for Rodney. "This was easy," he says, "I kept track of the hours and wages paid to my sons. They would take their payroll check to the bank, part was used for free spending (video games, etc.) and part was earmarked for savings. Once they had enough money saved up, they had a bank check drawn and filled out the brokerage form for the Roth-IRA. Voilà! They had opened their Roth IRA."

Rodney discusses money matters with his children all the time. Unlike opening the Roth IRA, that didn't start off too easy. It's dad and mom up against three typical all-American active boys. You might say Rodney didn't have a fighting chance, but that's exactly where he wanted his boys to be when the conversation started.

"When they were very young," he says, "I pushed concepts on them, saving versus spending. But investment concepts fly over the heads of children. They're more concerned about their video games and battles. So, I put investing concepts into their video game strategies. Before you can conquer the enemy, you must build your army first. One dollar represents a warrior. To build your army, you need a dividend paying stock which will create more dollars for you, which then increases the size of your army. Next, you need to train your warriors to fight and earn an upgrade. A trained warrior is stronger and more skillful, which provides a better opportunity to win. If you buy quality stocks to build your army, you are more likely to receive more dividends or earned capital gains vs. a non-quality stock which stagnates in price or doesn't increase dividends."

As they got older, the conversation relied less on the metaphor of the pixelated screen. For the Davis kids, the Child IRA came in baby steps (pun intended). "Before they opened their Roth IRAs," says Rodney, "I had opened regular brokerage accounts for them. I would discuss buying and selling stocks with them. Whenever, I come across an interesting article, I will forward the article web link to them."

They got into the groove as boys, but, as men, Alex, Ray, and Adam, can stay in the game with their father. "Now that they are adults," says Rodney, "when we talk on the phone, I will ask them 'What is new in their lives?' Remember, money doesn't buy love. Later on, at some point in the conversation, I will ask them about 'How are your investments doing?'"

Each son has developed his own personality when it comes to dealing with his IRA (and his dad). Rodney says, "My oldest son, Alex, who knows more than his father, takes an active role in decision making. For his accounts, he is the one who makes the buy and sell decisions. He and I have enjoyable conversations discussing investment strategy or how to allocate our investments for the future. He enjoys investing."

"My middle son, Ray, who knows more than his father, does not pay attention to his investments," says Rodney. "He is willing to let his father manage his investments. At this time, his focus is on his career and working long hours, so maybe things will change as he gets older or starts to raise his own family."

As he told us during his humorous story, Rodney says, "Adam, my polyurethane hero, is the risk taker in the family. He wants to chart his own course, but will listen to Dad once in a while. We'll discuss investment strategy and stocks to buy, but we don't always agree. Recently, he decided that he wanted to invest in Bitcoin, to the disagreement from his father. In the end, sometimes a teacher cannot instill the lesson to the pupil, sometimes the pupil has to learn the lesson for themselves from the School of Hard Knocks."

Speaking of the School of Hard Knocks, would Rodney have done anything differently based on what he now knows? "Life is always throwing new challenges at you," says Rodney. "With the downturn in the economy and college expenses, the Roth IRA plan for our kids was not executed as prescribed in the *Bottom Line* article (save $4,000 per year for 10 years). You cannot go back and change the past, so going forward I will strive to accomplish the Roth IRA plan for my kids (i.e., helping them save $4,000 a year for 10 years). Plus, I will continue to discuss & enlighten my kids on the value of managing their own finances & investments."

Rodney and Erica have prepared Alex, Ray, and Adam in ways no school can (perhaps other than that of Hard Knocks). The boys have investing experience and a financial planning perspective rarely found among their age group, or twice their age group for that matter. Therein lies the most important secret of the Child IRA. Sure, it can help your child retire in comfort, but that's not because the Child IRA grows seven digits (that's in the million dollar range for those nodding off). The real secret behind the Child IRA is that it helps put your child in the frame of mind that will allow your child to make proper choices regarding saving and investing for their retirement. As a result, they'll be better prepared to retire in comfort, no matter what happens to Social Security, company pension plans, or public policy.

Establishing a Child IRA benefits the next generation. Given its tremendous power, the Child IRA remains one of the most under-appreciated retirement savings tools available. In the remaining chapters, we'll present a virtual "how-to" manual that shows how different groups of people can implement and enjoy the advantages of the IRA. Feel free to start with the chapter that best represents the group you're in, but you might discover some ideas in reading the other chapters, too.

CHAPTER TWENTY-TWO:
FOR CHILDREN BELOW THE AGE OF 18

I f you're under the age of 18, this section is for you. But, before we get into some of the details of what you can and should be doing, I must congratulate you. The fact that you're reading this book tells me you have what it takes to be a winner in life. Winners plan ahead. Winners have no time for people who say, "you're too young to do this." Winners take control of their own lives and don't wait for someone to give them a helping hand. And, while this book is essentially about what you could do for yourself, these very traits will no doubt be noticed by colleges, employers, and your community. These attributes represent the qualities of leaders, and every organization wants leaders. They will be wanting you.

Believe it or not, in this great big country of ours, many young people have not learned the importance of demonstrating self-confidence. But quite a few have. As you begin to reach towards more competitive goals, you'll discover many like-minded peers who show these same characteristics.

Now, if you really want to *WOW!* colleges, employers, and your community, you'll want to show something more than just a drive and ambition to achieve. You'll actually want to show a list of real, practical, accomplishments. While the Child IRA will certainly count as an impressive feat, it will be the things you need to do in order to open and contribute to a Child IRA that will be the real feather in your cap. This chapter is about those things.

Remember, to contribute to a Child IRA, you'll need to earn income. The key word here is "earn." Money given as gifts doesn't count. Interest and dividends from investments don't count. Money that you find on the street won't count, either. You will need to go out and get a job. It can be any kind of job. You could deliver newspapers. You could sell lemonade on the sidewalk. Anything.

Here's the amazing thing: you are in a unique position to discover a business – or a way of doing business – that no one else has started yet. The fact is, you have an unfair advantage. You're too young to know the barriers and obstacles that might prevent you from pursuing an idea. This might sound bad but it's not. It's good. It means you can envision a path to success in a way no adult can.

You have another advantage. You're so young that you're still impressed by ten dollars. This might sound bad, but it's not. It's good. It means you're willing to start a small-scale operation that could grow larger. In contrast, adults might look at the same opportunity and say, "Why should I go through all that trouble just for ten dollars."

The biggest advantage you have, however, is your knowledge of your customers. You know kids in a way no adult can. This definitely is a good thing. You know what bothers you, what things you'd like to have, what games you like to play. Chances are, if you want these things, so do other kids your age. If you can make or provide those things, other kids will buy them. That's a really big advantage.

And age is not a restriction. If anything, age makes it easier, because the younger you are when you start, the easier it is for you to be successful (and the younger you'll be when you start your Child IRA!). The younger you are when you start your business, the fewer kids your age will also be starting businesses. That means less competition and a greater chance at making the money you need to contribute to your Child IRA.

There's one thing for sure: Age is not a barrier.

How do I know this? Because I've done this. I'm not just some old man using words to inspire you. I'm an old man who, as a young child, was inspired to make money. All I'm trying to do in this chapter is to share with you that same excitement I had as a kid entrepreneur.

Here's a few examples of what I did:

Towards the end of elementary school and into middle school (that's roughly the age of 11-13), my friends and I decided "kids like carnivals." So, for several days each summer for three years, we set up a carnival in our neighborhood. We made games for carnival-goers to play. We sold food we (or our mothers) made for our customers to buy. We even performed live action events for our visitors. That first year, we made seven dollars. That was a lot of baseball cards in those days. We were very excited with our success.

We figured we hit on a great idea, so the next year we added two new features. First, we included a movie presentation (we borrowed a Laurel and Hardy movie from the local library) and we converted a portion of my friend's walk-in basement into a fun house. That year we made eleven dollars. This excited us even more.

The year-over-year growth of more than 50% inspired us to extend both our offerings and our marketing efforts that third year. Rather than borrowing a movie from the library, we made a short (five minute) movie involving those little plastic army men, stop-action photography, and lots of (innocent) pyrotechnics. I was the cameraman. I was a pretty bad cameraman, but everyone got a kick out of the movie.

I was much better, however, when it came to leading the improved marketing campaign. In the first two years of the carnival, we focused only on the kids in our small neighborhood. We had a handful of much larger neighborhoods around us. That's who I marketed the carnival to in the third year.

On the opening day of the carnival, I was nervous. I didn't know if anyone from outside our neighborhood would come. Rather than sitting back and waiting, I got on my bike and rode to the neighborhoods to remind all the kids. In one of the neighborhoods, all the kids had already left for the carnival. There was about two dozen in the group. They were the first to arrive at the carnival (when I wasn't there). One of my friends who was helping with the carnival thought it would be funny to tell them the carnival was over, so those kids left and never came back. They had all this money to spend, but didn't, because somebody wanted to make a joke. It turns out that joke wasn't too funny and really hurt us.

We did have other neighborhood's kids come, and that third (and final) year we nearly doubled the previous year's take with a gross revenue of twenty-one dollars – even without those two dozen kids who came and left! This was our last year because it was evident everyone didn't approach the carnival with the same level of seriousness. This is what happens when you go into business with partners. If you're not all on the same page, if you don't all agree on the same goals, the venture will break apart.

That was OK, because I used those neighborhood contacts to start my next venture. I didn't make any money on this one, but I had a lot of fun. You see, back in those days, it was very difficult to play organized football. Sure, there was Pop Warner and Vince Lombardi football, but it was very expensive and usually inconvenient to join those leagues. Instead, we played sandlot football on our street. Kids in each neighborhood would play pick-up games in their respective neighborhoods. And that would be that.

Not quite, though. When it comes to sports, kids like to brag about their abilities. Each neighborhood would brag that it had the best team. There was no way to prove it, of course, because the neighborhoods never played against each other.

That's when I had my great idea to form a neighborhood football league. I would arrange game schedules. We'd go play at local elementary schools. Those were the only fields big enough for our teams. It was still sandlot football. This meant there were no referees – we had to learn how to play fair by ourselves. It also meant there were no parents – we had to rely on our own devices to get to and from the playing fields. Most important, it meant there was no game clock. We'd just play until dark. Our league gave each neighborhood a chance to prove its bragging rights.

I'm happy to report our neighborhood never lost a game.

But the really great business idea occurred during the era of the neighborhood football league and really blossomed into my high school years. This was the mid-1970s and sports card collecting was about to go mainstream. My brother and I anticipated this (or were just lucky with our timing) and started a baseball card/football card dealership before any kids knew the meaning of the term. This was the age when most of our peers were turning away from collecting baseball cards and moving on to other things. As a result, they were more than willing to sell their cards to us in bulk (in other words, we didn't have to pay that much money for their cards).

Still young enough to know what our peers wanted (money for their cards), we were also old enough to set up tables at adult card shows and sell our cards to both kids and adults. We soon learned how to get cards directly from the manufacturer. At its peak, this business made a few thousand dollars a year. That was more than enough for me and my brother. It also shows what happens when two partners are in total agreement with how the business should be run. Unfortunately for us, we didn't know about IRAs at that point in our life because Congress had just created the law.

My stories are decades old. The world of kid business has changed – dramatically! Today, it's easier for teens and pre-teens to start their own business. First, parents are more accepting of their kids starting businesses (since the 1980s, our country has taken on a much more entrepreneurial flavor). Second, the kids themselves are more quickly immersed into business and finance because they can see so many examples through the internet and social media (not to mention video games). Finally, again because of the internet and social media, there has never been a time of greater opportunity for kids to develop their own business. I'll end this chapter with a dozen examples of kids as young as five who have started their own businesses. Take a look at these and see if they can inspire an idea or two in your own head.

Elementary School Entrepreneurs

Ken & Kate's Snow Cones.
Shantae Pelt, Founder of Coco'Pie Clothing in Gilbert, Arizona, has two daughters who created an LLC for Ken & Kate's Snow Cones. Mikayla started the business at age 9 along with her sister Kennedy who was then five-years-old. Shantae describes the girls' venture as a "Snow Cone Business operated via a snow cone cart on wheels. They use a machine capable of crushing 500lbs of ice per hour and a variety of

cane sugar syrups at the customer's choice. Each Snow Cone cost $1 and tips are highly encouraged."

The idea came to the sisters much the same way the carnival idea came to me and my friends. After visiting a food festival and noticing a shaved ice vendor New Orleans Style Shaved Ice, Mikayla was inspired to start a similar business. After asking Mom to help, they've been pushing along for more than two years now.

The girls have learned that everything isn't very easy. For example, Mikayla had to re-design her snow cone cart several times. Shantae says "She also learned how to give great customer service and encourage people to buy. Kennedy has learned that she can't continue to eat all of the profits, and, also, that she can't use money the business has made to purchase her own snow cones!"

You can imagine how successful selling cool, refreshing, snow cones in the hot Arizona climate can be. Mix in this the novelty of two elementary school children operating the business, and you have a great head start into the business world. Very rapidly, they found their mother's friends began inviting them to set up their cart at area events. As word spread, local media picked up the story. Mikayla and Kennedy soon appeared on *Sonoran Living* (which airs on the ABC affiliate). This led to both increased confidence and visibility.

Shantae adds the girls learned much from organizations designed to help child entrepreneurs. "The Arizona Children's Business Fair taught them about profit, cost, and how to pitch," she says. "It also showed them why it's important to keep selling – even on slow days – to just keep going, and keep looking for new opportunities."

HorseCrazyGirls.com

"Teenpreneur" Sydney Englund started her business at the age of nine and has been operating it for nearly a decade. HorseCrazyGirls.com is a website where "horse-crazy" girls can share their love of horses. They can share their favorite books, movies, their artwork, stories, and find plenty of horse games. It receives over 26,000 visitors a month from around the world."

"Being a young horse-obsessed girl, I wanted a place where I could not only share my love of horses, but also nurture it," says Sydney. "There was no website that offered everything I was looking for so I started my own."

She remembers "being super excited when I started my business. I wanted to put everything and anything on my site. That was not the best plan and ran into problems, including getting penalized by Google. I have had to do a lot of work to get the website performing well again. There have been a lot of ups and downs. I've tried things that worked surprisingly well and some that didn't, but everything I've done has taught me something about being an entrepreneur."

Sydney's business is going so strong she is getting ready to launch her own products. "I believe my passion for horses and great resources for horsecrazy girls is what has made my business successful," she says.

KidNewsMaker

Alejandra Stack is the CEO/Founder/Reporter of KidNewsMaker, based in the greater Atlanta, Georgia area, specifically, Carrollton, Georgia. Alejandra began her first newspaper column (in the *Florida Star* and *Georgia Star*) when she was eight years old. "I get my nose for news from my mom and she took me in the newsroom for the first time when I was three weeks old," says Alejandra. "She's a single mom so when she didn't have a sitter, she'd bring me along and I got to meet lots of people like celebrities, politicians, and other important people. They'd talk to me and I'd talk back. People called me "Allie in Action" and told my mom I was a natural. One night she was working late for the elections and told me to go read something so she could work. I noticed the only stories in their papers were of kids who were doing crimes or doing sports. So I told her they need to show positive stuff on kids if they want kids to read the paper. She told me to go write a story and I wrote three."

By age 9 or 10, "Allie in Action" started making videos. She also had completed a kidprenuer business course and met tons of great kids and felt they should be highlighted. She used money she had made working on a film to start KidNewsMaker when she was 11. She has since won three journalism awards.

"My company is a kid-centric multi-media platform," says Alejandra. "KidNewsMaker consists of online, print, and video interviews with kids making major moves across various platforms. My motto is 'We're not waiting, we're creating.' I don't want to just show celebrities because not everyone can be that. I want kids to be inspired by seeing people in their community or school or whatever accomplish attainable goals."

When she started her company, Alejandra took advantage of a local program for kids. It taught her a lot about marketing. "I was known as 'Allie in Action' and so I had to learn about rebranding and creating a campaign that was attractive to viewers," she says. "Through the ExCel Youth Mentorship Program, I learned many aspects of starting a business and being consistent. The course was taught by my mentor, Gabrielle Jordan, a teen who travels the world and gives motivational speeches. My mom joined a Momager Academy to learn how to balance this stuff for me."

Social media has made KidNewsMaker successful, along with her going from backstage baby to being the one asking the questions. Alejandra has gotten endorsements from local government leaders, youth and church organizations, and now is going international including kids from the United Kingdom and Caribbean.

Of course, it doesn't hurt that her mother is Arthia Nixon, an award-winning journalist, publicist, publisher, media personality, author, and communications coach/consultant. "First off, as a parent I am thrilled she has chosen to follow my path at such an early age," says Arthia. "The thing is, she is carving her own niche early on and giving people an insight into the future leaders of tomorrow. I'm a single mom and things are tough but through this, she has inspired me to even go back to school and do business courses to ensure that I am representing her properly as a mom and COO/Managing Editor. I used to see it as a hobby, but now she's got investors interested and this is a business. I'm thrilled."

Middle School Entrepreneurs

Used Golf Ball Sales

Not all business ideas need be elaborate. Some can be very simple. In fact, simple business ideas are often the most successful. Why? Because they don't require a lot of effort to start and it's easy for customers to see the benefits. Mario Cruz, a marketing manager for a spill containment company in Jacksonville, Florida says his 12-year old son had one of those simple ideas when he "started selling golf balls at the 14th hole of the golf course we live on."

Proximity prompted this pre-teen to begin his business venture. "We live on a golf course but no one in our family plays golf," says Mario. "We collected the golf balls that landed in our pool and yard just for the fun of it to see how many we could get. One day, he emptied the vases that we had put them in, put them in his backpack and walked onto the course to 'set up shop'."

Golfers tend to share certain traits and they were impressed by this boy's ingenuity. "Presumably, the people that play golf are successful and have worked hard to get there," says Mario. "There are countless stories of people who are very impressed with my son and his business savvy. Some who aren't 'in the market' for golf balls will give him cash and/or buy him a drink or snack to show their appreciation for his efforts. One gentleman, after learning that my son will go into the ponds to fish balls out of the water gave him his ball retriever to make it easier."

Grom Social

Growing up on the Indian River Lagoon along Florida's Space Coast, it's easy to understand how Zach Marks and his family became surfing enthusiasts. Living in the shadows of the place that literally launched America's greatest achievement – the Apollo "Man on the Moon" project – it's also not surprising that Zach, Founder of Grom Social, would feel no task is too ambitious.

Ambition fuels curiosity. Curiosity, in turn, inspires you to explore. Sometimes exploration reveals great discoveries. Other times, exploration leads you into areas that can get you in trouble. If you're lucky, that trouble leads you to one of those great discoveries. Such is the story of the journey that inspired Zach to create Grom Social.

"I was 11-years-old and had a secret Facebook account with a few hundred friends," says Zach. "My dad (Darren) caught me and made me stop using Facebook as I was too young. I once again sneaked onto Facebook and was once again caught by my dad. This time, he jokingly told me to go start my own social media network if I wanted to use one so badly."

They say necessity is the mother of invention, and, if Zach wanted to enjoy the "Facebook experience," it would be necessary for him to invent a way to do so. Enter "Grom Social," and the rest, as they say, is history. "I have always been a computer enthusiast and learned a lot about coding," says Zach. "I brainstormed a lot of ideas with my siblings, my parents, and my friends. Soon enough, we were ready to launch the platform. We named it Grom Social because 'grom' is slang for a young surfer. Our whole family loves to surf."

There's nothing like the excitement of breathing life into a new business. Of course, if you think that's exciting, imagine what it's like to see that business begin to take off. "It was exhilarating," says Zach. "The idea clicked right away. Once we were ready to launch, we told our friends and their families. They then told their friends and family. We just saw the amount of people signing up to use Grom Social grow and grow and grow. The numbers ballooned even more after we received attention on *USA Today*. It was so unexpected, but it was also just a lot of fun. I woke up excited each day to check to see how many more people were using the site and what people were saying about Grom Social."

What does Zach say about Grom Social? "Grom Social is a social media network that's 'for kids by kids' used by children between the ages of 5-16," he says. "Grom Social is filled with wonderful interactive games and videos that are both fun and educational, and in particular emphasizes good digital citizenship. In addition, Grom Social is the safest social media network for children as it allows parents/guardians to monitor their kids' usage on the site."

Zach was 11-years-old when he started the business. Today he and his family live in San Juan Capistrano, California. He's moved to the next phase of his life, and so has Grom Social. "I'm 17 now and have just started my freshman year of college," says the young entrepreneur. "The business is still operating. In fact, we just became a publicly traded company. Today, Grom Social has about 12 million users and trades as GRMM on the OTCBB. The key to the success of the company was all of the hard work we put into it. My dad is a great influence on me. So are my siblings. We just constantly come up with new and more ideas to make the site grow. We make it fun for us. And what's fun for us is also fun for the other kids who use the site."

Frilliance

Like many her age, Fiona Frills of Saratoga, California, loves YouTube. In fact, she loves it so much she started her own YouTube channel when she was only 10 years old. She began posting a series she called "Gross Food." She developed quite a following.

In the meantime, she was fascinated with makeup. When she was 12 she decided to follow a path she had seen other YouTubers take. She noticed they promoted and sold products. Fiona thought this would be fun to try. She combined her two loves and – presto! – she created Frilliance, a brand of cosmetics and makeup tools for teens.

Fiona started the makeup brushes and tools line because she loves makeup and fashion. She posts videos about makeup. Almost half a million people subscribe to her YouTube channel. That gives her a large ready-made audience to pitch her products to.

Now 14, Fiona is still running the business today. She knows it takes a lot of patience to work through all the details of business. She's discovered making everything come together for a business requires much more than she thought. She credits the success of Frilliance on her passion and love for makeup and beauty, so she feels like it isn't that much work.

AfterLite BodyCare

If anyone can create their own TV channel on YouTube, they can create their own store on Etsy. That's exactly what Destiny Helligar of Burbank, California did. Destiny, the CEO of AfterLite Bath and Bodycare Company, discovered the bodycare products she was using were very harsh on her skin. "I realized that I wasn't the only person with this problem, so I started to make natural soaps," says the pre-teen entrepreneur.

It wasn't easy to start. Destiny says, "I remember all the hard work you put into making the product and how many times you have to fail before you get a product right." Today, Destiny offers a full line of products through her all-natural bath body company. "We sell all-natural soaps, bath bombs, deodorant, and whipped oils," she says.

Destiny believes her company will remain vibrant because "we market to fix common skin problems."

Laine Avenue Backpacks

Emily Laine Miller of Columbus, Ohio was 13 years old and she had a problem. She actually had two problems. Like many entrepreneurs, she used one problem to solve the other. In doing so, she not only helped herself, she helped others who faced the same challenges she did.

"From an early age my parents have always taught me the importance of saving money for college," says Emily. "But as a busy teen, it was hard to find a part-time job that worked with my schedule. So, I came up with the idea to start a business that would help me earn money for college and also solve another problem my friends and I faced each year: finding a backpack that was stylish and functional, and that would stand up to the wear and tear from school and activities. I also thought it would be cool to find a way to change up the look of my backpack throughout the year."

Getting an idea for a product is only the first step. If you want that product to be successful, you need to talk to the people who you expect to buy the product before you start making it. That's what Emily did. In the process, she discovered she wasn't alone in her problems. Many of her friends had similar concerns. Her initial simple idea of a single physical product (the backpack) became a very broad solution for her intended market. It would also help her sell that product.

"Once I started talking to my friends about the idea, I realized so many teens like me also struggled to find a part-time job and save money for college," says Emily. "So, I had the idea to set up the company so other teens (in partnership with a parent) can sign up to be a Laine Avenue Backer and earn 25% commission on every backpack sold. It's really providing an alternative to the traditional part-time job and giving teens the opportunity to learn about entrepreneurship. Our online Life Skills Academy also teaches skills not always taught in high school, like financial management, personal development, and family and relationships. We really want to help teens and young adults learn all the skills needed to be successful in the future."

It took a few years to get all the kinks out, but Emily officially launched the business in the spring of 2017. Now sixteen, she says, "Laine Avenue backpacks are the only backpacks on the market that can be customized through an interchangeable zipper flap, making it easy for teens to have a backpack to match every mood. The backpacks are made with durable brushed cotton and an ergonomic design that can carry up to three 3-inch binders, plus a laptop, folders and notebooks—holding everything needed for school. Laine Avenue convertible backpacks also include a detachable cross-body purse for carrying small essentials."

Knowing that she's helping herself and helping others obviously makes Emily feel good. There's nothing more satisfying than success. "One of the coolest parts about the business is seeing kids at my school who I don't even know wearing a Laine Avenue backpack, or getting an order in from across the country," says Emily. "We only sell online and through our network of Backers, so word of mouth and social media has been key in getting the word out about my company. We've been lucky to get some great media attention. Seeing my backpacks featured on *The Today Show* was also a favorite moment."

Emily understands how much work it takes to launch a business. She appreciates all the help she's received, and is happy that she can return the favor to others. She says, "Operating a business is hard, but I'm lucky to have the support of my parents, family and friends. We're continuing to think about new products and designs to offer and other ways to get the word out about not only the backpacks, but the opportunity we are offering teens to earn money and gain life skills."

High School Entrepreneurs

Relaxing Meditations

Chris James, Co-founder of relaxingmeditations.com in Ames, Iowa, is just what you'd expect in a boy from America's heartland. He served as Senior Patrol Leader for his Boy Scout Troop. He has helped unload trucks for the local church's food shelf. And he loves his mother. More on that last thing in a moment.

Today he is a 19-year-old student at Iowa State University where he's working on a Bachelor's Degree in Entrepreneurship and Marketing. To give you a sense of his dynamic nature, he won first place in the ISU Spring Innovative Pitch Competition and received a $12,000 grant as part of the colleges "Cystarters Program" – a 10-week long business incubator for active entrepreneurs.

The story of Chris' entrepreneurial zeal begins in high school. He undertook several projects, in the creation of a comedy YouTube channel as well as various successful blogs. He also developed an app that was dubbed "Tinder for Kittens and Puppies." But it was his mother's work that inspired Chris to start his first business when he was 15 years old. "Two things prompted me to start," says Chris. "The first was I wanted to retire my mom. She works so hard for my family and I knew this would be a good way to make a passive income (though again, I had no idea what that meant at the time). The second was I thought it would be cool to make money online."

What was it exactly that Chris did while still in his early high school years? "My mom is a clinical hypnotist meaning she helps people lose weight, stop smoking and release a variety of limitations," recalls Chris. "She was currently only making money by having people come into her office and receive a CD version of the session. Although she made good money doing it, I knew if she converted those CD's to MP3's she could sell online to virtually anyone in the world and it would be scalable. (At the time I didn't know of the word 'scalable,' but the way I described it to her was if I placed her program online it would cost just as much, and take up just as much energy to sell to 1 person or to 1 million people. This just so happens to be the definition of 'scalable'). So, me, being the naïve teenager and knowing nothing about internet marketing, asked if I could sell her MP3's online."

Chris targeted really niche areas with smaller audiences, such as horseback riders who lost their confidence and it eventually turned into relaxingmeditations.com. "It went terrible at first," he says, "and I ended up burning up a lot of her cash, but I kept experimenting and eventually we started making a profit. I remember when I first started I'd spend $100 on ads, and only make a $10 sale. I had no clue what I was doing, but I kept learning."

Starting any business, but especially your first business, quickly dispels those naïve notions we all have. "I thought it would be super easy, but instead it was insanely difficult," says Chris. "I'd think, 'all right, all I have to do is place this online and it will sell itself.' Wrong. I thought I'd run some ads for the business and if only 5% converted, I make 200% profit. Only ½% converted and I lost money. It's just hurdle after hurdle. It really humbled me in that aspect."

Thanks to the support of his mother, Chris weathered those first inevitable hurdles. "What made it successful was that I kept going," he says. "My mom kept throwing cash at it. She knew I was getting a valuable education out of this experience. No matter what setbacks I pushed through, tried something new, ran another experiment and raised my margins."

According to the website, Relaxing Meditations has helped more than 5,000 people. And at $149 a pop, simple math tells you Chris has helped his mom's business bring in more than three-quarters of a million dollars in revenue. Now that's what we call a good way to measure success!

Hygee Phone

Bennett Cohen, C.E.O & C.B.B (Chief Bacteria Buster) of Hygee, LLC, quickly assimilated into his new school after moving from Maryland to Malibu, California. He played varsity tennis, became part of the Mock Trial team, and joined the Model United Nations club, all the while earning a spot on the school's honor roll. Bennett's mom Jill says, "Like most teens, Bennett's phone is almost a 5th appendage! But when he found out how germ filled they are and how those germs can cause acne he set out to create a product that reduces that."

"I've always been a bit of a germaphobe, and research showed me that cell phones are the single grossest thing we use on a daily basis," says Bennett. "Studies show that phones are 10x-18x dirtier than public toilets and contain harmful bacteria such as E. coli, MRSA, and Staph. In short, phones can cause disease and gross acne (acne was a big part for me). Think about it, you bring your phone to work, on the metro, to the gym, but never really clean it. I knew alcohol kills germs, but turns out it is super bad for the phone, and can damage the electronics."

Shortly after turning 17, Bennett began working on a product to help alleviate this problem. "Hygee, LLC (hygeephone.com) is a tech-healthcare company that sells antibacterial phone cases and an antibacterial screen polish/cleaner," says Bennett. ("Hygee" is a play on the word "hygiene.")

Given that Bennett created a physical product (as opposed to an internet or media-based service), he discovered a different set of hurdles on the way to obtaining a patent. He says his most memorable experiences include "the months spent just prototyping the case and attempting to apply the natural mineral solution to the case permanently. That was one of the hardest things to accomplish regarding the product. I've also exhibited Hygee at startup conventions, which have helped me grow as a presenter and understand the world of business much better."

Bennett also learned the importance of working with well recognized institutions to gain both credibility and government approval. "We've partnered with leading green chemists to create coatings that have been scientifically supported by the University of Florida, the University of Leeds, and NASA," says the website he created for the product. In addition, Bennett has sought and obtained approval of his product from the U.S. Food and Drug Administration.

Like almost every entrepreneur, any short conversation about his business immediately reveals Bennett's passion. "The sheer penetration of the issue has made this something that everyone can relate to," he says. "Nearly everyone has a smartphone, and 92% of people use their phone in the bathroom. Ew! Hygee solves the serious issue of germs on phones for everyone, ranging from teens with acne to parents letting toddlers use their phones to the public transport commuter."

His mom sees it, too. "I am constantly amazed by Bennett's hard work and commitment to Hygee Phone," says Jill. "Now, if he would clean his room and make his bed every now and then instead of calling chemists all over the world and working on product design that would be great!"

Junior Achievement

High school students interested in creating a business but don't have a specific product or service in mind might want to explore school or community-based programs specifically geared for this purpose. For example, Tara Nolan, Marketing Manager of Junior Achievement of Northern New England in Waltham, Massachusetts, tells us her group offers its program to students aged 14-18 years old.

Tara and her colleague Phil Symons, (Program Manager at Junior Achievement of Northern New England), shared a recent experience they've had with teenagers who created their own company. "Vibes Inc. was founded in 2017 by a group of students from Boston and Greater Boston who came together through the JA Academy program," says Tara. "Their signature product, the Hearmuff, infused high powered headphone speakers with comfortable and warm behind-the-head earmuffs offering maximum comfort."

Tara explains how Vibes, Inc. came about. "These students participated in our organization's signature entrepreneurship program, the JA Academy Program," she says. "This 13-week program allows students to create, operate, and liquidate their own company. They create a product that satisfies a community need, then they market and sell this product to a target audience. They raise real capital to fund the venture, all while learning how to operate a business using our blended learning platform, where this program's online curriculum is housed."

The beauty of an established program like Junior Achievement is that teens can quickly realize what aspect of business and entrepreneurial activity most excites them. "Students' experiences varied in what they remember most, but all felt that this program significantly changed their lives," says Tara. "One exciting moment for everyone involved was when the group was invited to compete in the Junior Achievement National Leadership Summit – out of 100+ Junior Achievement chapters, Vibes Inc. was one of only 15 student companies chosen to participate in the competition."

While businesses created in these programs tend to be ad hoc and/or short-lived, that doesn't mean there's no measure of success. "The business is no longer in operation, but the success of the business was marked by their sales numbers as well as the group dynamic," says Tara. "Another success that Vibes Inc. saw was the second-place title at a Babson College business competition, beating out several other high school and college companies."

Child entrepreneurialism represents one of the most fulfilling ways to earn the income necessary to establish a Child IRA. For all these examples, though, the most likely path for most families is for the child to work for someone else. We explore this avenue in the next chapter.

CHAPTER TWENTY-THREE:
FOR PARENTS AND GRANDPARENTS

Before she became a teenager, Baylee Morrison had released her first single, starred in TV commercials, and made nearly two hundred appearances, including on a prime-time television episode and singing the National Anthem three times for the NFL's Buffalo Bills. In many ways, Baylee represents the path many parents help guide their young children towards. As often happens, the path begins with a genuine interest in entertaining, and not necessarily a way to earn income. Let's take a closer look at how this young actress/singer/dancer/model traveled along her path.

"Baylee was first interested in singing when she used to sing in the car on the way home from school in the back of her grandparents' car," says Bonnie Morrison, Baylee's mom. "Once, while on a family vacation, her grandpa took her down to the restaurant where they were having a karaoke night. Baylee sang a few songs and fell in love with the feeling of performing and making people smile when they listened to her sing. After attending several different child theater workshops when she was 7 years old, she had a few different vocal coaches. She has had her current vocal coach for the past 4 years. Baylee's first paying job was a commercial for Stickley furniture when she was 7 years old."

Although singing might have been Baylee's entrée into the entertainment world, it led to modeling and acting. Those two activities, in turn, led to her first paycheck. To get there, her path took her, temporarily, to Los Angeles. "While in LA, she was a fit model for Forever 21 for three months," says Bonnie. "She has been in a few commercials and appeared on an episode of *The Bacherlorette*. Baylee has received payment for the commercials she was in, the episode of *The Bachelorette* she was in, and when she modeled for Forever 21."

As with most other situations where a child gets paid, it's necessary to obtain and file the proper forms. "You have to have a child performing work permit to have your child work and earn money," says Bonnie. "Baylee had a child performer work permit while we were in LA and currently holds a child performer work permit in New York. You can download a form and mail in the necessary paperwork. You have to renew every year."

Baylee performs all the time, but usually only accepts donations toward her college fund. She deposits all these donations into a custodial account. Sometimes, she uses the funds to cover expenses and further her career. "Funds are put toward her future college plans, but some of the money is also used to work on her skills for her career (singing, dancing, acting, and modeling lessons)," says Bonnie.

When she was 12, Baylee released her debut single "Discommunication" on iTunes and Spotify. She soon found out this threw a bit of a monkey wrench into her plans. "We were trying to keep her as an amateur for singing so she could compete in events," says Bonnie. "She wasn't looking for paying gigs, she was just singing because she loves it!" Shortly after releasing the song, Baylee found out her path had changed. "When she went to compete at the New York State Fair, somebody told them she wasn't an amateur anymore," says Bonnie. "Now we will be looking for paying gigs! (in my spare time, which I have none of). I guess since she released a song on iTunes, she is no longer an amateur, even though she only makes pennies on the dollar! Baylee is hoping to start performing at birthday parties, charity events, sports events, and other events in the near future and receive payment for her performances."

Baylee Morrison began her journey when she was only seven years old. In six years she's accomplished plenty, but there's more to go. At the time of writing, she's getting ready to shoot a music video of "Discommunication." In addition, she has another original song ready for the recording studio. "It is a tough business for sure!" says Bonnie. "There is a huge learning curve! We'll be again traveling to LA for her to perform in front of agents and managers and hoping at some point she gets her break. She works hard and deserves a break!"

Bonnie Morrison has taken a very active role in the development of her daughter's childhood career. At the time she was interviewed for this book, setting up a Child IRA wasn't in the forefront of her mind.

*   *   *   *   *

Congratulations! If you're reading this chapter that means you're an upbeat parent or grandparent seeking to give your children or grandchildren the benefit of your life's experience. At one point or another, we've all lamented "if only I knew then what I know now." While you can't anticipate every possible situation that may relate to the lifetime of your child, you can address one of these many items right now: your child's retirement. What parent or grandparent wouldn't want to help their child or grandchild become a millionaire by the time that child retires? Establishing a Child IRA can accomplish this.

Here's how to do it.

These three easy-to-understand steps will help start you (and your child) on the way. While the previous chapter focused on kids who took the initiative to create their own businesses, this chapter is for proactive parents who want to help place their children in a position to establish a Child IRA. As you can tell from Bonnie Morrison's experience, it's possible to start a child on this journey early in life, but you need to be prepared for long hours and hard work. The impetus to encourage a child to start a Child IRA goes well beyond the prospects of retiring in comfort. "Much like anything a parent tries to teach a child along the lines of good habits, saving for the future is important," says Maura Cassidy. "Saving in a tax-advantaged account may make sense for you and your children."

Step #1: Assess Risks

Parents need to be aware of several considerations before agreeing to let their minor children earn an income. First and foremost, among them are the potential tax consequences. "Parents need to know the tax code states a child/dependent cannot provide more than 50% of their own support," says Suzanne Weathers. If the intention is to earn only enough income to contribute to the Child IRA, however, it's unlikely this 50% threshold will be met.

Beyond taxes, there are the usual concerns when it comes to activities outside of school. "Deciding to work before you are 18 is a huge time commitment that takes time away from your schoolwork," says Evelyn Cook. "The most important question to ask is whether that sacrifice is worth the additional income."

Speaking of school, as the child approaches college age, earned income may have a material impact on financial aid packages. Scott Vance, "Probably a big thing to think about is college funding. The income of a child is included in the financial aid computations at a much higher rate than a parent's income. The data for computing financial aid has recently changed now so that when the child is a sophomore in high school, their tax situation is used to compute their freshman year of college financial aid eligibility."

The college equation continues beyond high school and into the child's college years. This potentially presents "a more complicated situation for parents of college age students who may receive partial scholarships, making this the perfect time for these parents and students to meet with a tax professional for a full review of how these changes may impact the bottom-line come tax time," says Weathers.

Step #2: Identify Opportunities

Once parents determine it makes sense for their children to begin earning the income necessary to contribute to a Child IRA, it's important to become familiar with Child Labor Laws. Chapter 18 reviewed some important points. Here are a few more.

While it's easiest for the child if the parents own their own business (we'll discuss this special circumstance in the next chapter), this is not an essential condition. "Owning your own business is not necessary to set up an IRA for your child," says Jose Silva, Founder & CEO of Silva Fiduciary Advisors in Daytona Beach and Orlando, Florida. "As long as they have some kind of income – whether it be from yardwork, babysitting, walking the dog, or whatever – young people can start their own IRA and, if minors, their parents can set the IRA up as custodian or guardian for them."

Beyond these traditional jobs, and before you jump into positions that can generate substantial income, it's important to review important rules regarding the employment of minors. Ryan Neumeyer, says, "The federal child labor provisions, also known as the child labor laws, are authorized by the Fair Labor Standards Act (FLSA) of 1938. All states have child labor standards. When Federal and state standards are different, the rules that provide the most protection to young workers will apply. The FLSA, subject to a few exceptions, confines the employment of 14- and 15-year-olds to:

- Employment after school unless through school sponsored programs to three hours or less during a school day.
- Eight hours or less on non-school days.
- 18 hours a week or less during school weeks.
- 40 hours or less during non-school weeks."

Neumeyer adds, "At 16 years of age, youth may be employed for unlimited hours in any non-agricultural occupation other than one declared to be hazardous by the Secretary of Labor. Hazardous occupations are as follows:

- Manufacturing and storing of explosives.
- Motor-vehicle driving and outside helper on a motor vehicle.
- Coal mining.
- Occupations in forest fire fighting, forest fire prevention, timber tract operations, forestry service, logging, and sawmilling.
- Power-driven woodworking machines.
- Exposure to radioactive substances.
- Power-driven hoisting apparatus, including forklifts.
- Power-driven metal-forming, punching, and shearing machines.
- Mining, other than coal mining.

- Operating power-driven meat processing equipment, including meat slicers and other food slicers, in retail establishments (such as grocery stores, restaurants, kitchens, and delis) and wholesale establishments, and most occupations in meat and poultry slaughtering, packing, processing, or rendering.
- Power-driven bakery machines including vertical dough or batter mixers.
- Power-driven balers, compactors, and paper processing machines.
- Manufacturing bricks, tile, and kindred products.
- Power-driven circular saws, bandsaws, chain saws, guillotine shears, wood chippers, and abrasive cutting discs.
- Wrecking, demolition, and shipbreaking operations.
- Roofing operations and all work on or about a roof.
- Excavation operations."

The good news, according to Neumeyer, is that certain businesses (family-owned) and industries (modeling, acting) are exempt from some of these guidelines. He lists these (and what guidelines are they not exempt from) as follows:

- There are various exemptions under the FLSA's prohibitions on labor for children in agriculture work on family owned farms and with the consent of the parent for a child to work on farms.
- Children 16 and 17 years of age employed by their parents in occupations other than those declared hazardous by the Secretary of Labor are exempt under the FLSA.
- Children under 16 years of age employed by their parents in occupations other than manufacturing or mining, or occupations declared hazardous by the Secretary of Labor are exempt.
- The FLSA exempts performers and actors from the child labor rules.
- Newspaper delivery boys/girls are exempt.

Do some of these exemptions look familiar? Are you beginning to get a better idea of what's possible for your children? Still, there remains one overriding consideration all parents must be aware of before allowing their child to work for someone else. "The number one concern should be safety," says Neumeyer. "If an employer is willing to have a child work in a business, it should have policies and procedures to keep them safe. You should request a copy of all policies and procedures. Companies should, at a minimum, have an employee handbook which includes safety rules, or a separate safety manual. Determine if there will be adult supervision while the child is working or if the child will be left alone. Inspect the place of employment and interview the manager regarding what is expected and the job duties. Observe an employee actually performing the proposed job to determine if there are any safety risks. Contact OSHA and inquire whether there have been any violations by the employer. A parent can also search the local court docket and bureau of workers compensation to determine if there has been an inordinate amount of accidents. While there are no steps that will absolutely shield your child from every potential harm, by simply going through the aforementioned steps you can better protect your child in the work place."

Step 3: Start Saving in a Child IRA

Chapter 16 outlines various ways you can set up a Child IRA. You can do this at most major financial institutions. Just speak to your favorite bank, broker, or mutual fund. They should have ready-made instructions for you to establish a Child IRA (they often call it a "custodial" or "minor child" IRA). You can complete this part of the process as soon as your child earns that first paycheck.

Now, if your child is like any other child, the money earned will quickly be spent on items for immediate gratification or placed in a college savings fund. Neither of these are particularly bad options as the former helps teach the importance of financial management (i.e., budgeting) and the latter helps build responsible financial behavior through long-term goal setting. Still, neither one allows the child's earnings to be contributed to a Child IRA. That's where the parents (and grandparents) can lend a hand.

Remember, the rule for contributing to a Child IRA is that the income be earned. That income can be used for anything. It doesn't have to be saved for contributing to the Child IRA. The actual money used for the Child IRA contribution can come from somewhere else. Like the parents or grandparents. Yes, parents and grandparents can help establish Child IRAs "simply by funding the IRA or Roth IRA for the child who has earnings," says Timothy Shanahan, CEO, Compass Capital Corporation in Braintree, Massachusetts.

This can be as straightforward as giving it a part of a birthday present (talk about a gift that keeps on giving). "It's easy to do, but grandparents need to be certain their grandchildren have earned income to do this," says Ted Jenkin.

It's important, though, for parents and grandparents to synchronize any gifting for the purposes of contributing to a Child IRA. Marianela Collado, says, "Similar to parents, grandparents can help fund the IRAs. They'll need to make sure they coordinate with the parents as to avoid over funding. The max is limited to their earned income or $5,500. We can't forget that."

Beyond gifts, grandparents can help by "communicating and encouraging their children to participate given the many benefits – educational and financial – for their grandkids," says Silva.

It may entail a unit of work for parents to help their kids find meaningful income opportunities. If the parents have a family owned business, however, that effort becomes much easier, as we will see in the next chapter.

CHAPTER TWENTY-FOUR:
FOR FAMILY OWNED BUSINESSES

Following his graduation from Missouri State University, Gabe Lumby of Springfield, Missouri did what most folks who major in accounting and finance do. For nearly six years he worked in various positions for other accounting firms, methodically advancing in his career. Then it dawned on him. He had grown enough where it made sense for him to have his own firm. So, in July 2015, he hung his name on a shingle and began directly servicing the kinds of small businesses he had served for years. At the same time, a couple years later, he decided to help his younger brother Jacob by taking on an additional role as Chief Marketing Officer at Jacob's firm Cash Cow Couple. Jacob and Vanessa Gumby's website shares the lessons learned by the husband and wife team. The popular personal financial blog, while geared to young couples like Jacob and Vanessa, overlaps nicely with Gabe's niche – small business owners.

Gabe's accounting experience taught him several important lessons for running his business. Among the most important, however, was establishing IRAs as early as possible. This included not only his own retirement savings, but also a Child IRA for his son. "I didn't personally setup an IRA for myself (nor did my parents) before I was 18," says Lumby, "but I have done so for one of my kids and this is a tax strategy I recommend and help implement for clients."

Unlike other parents, families who own their own businesses have a distinct advantage when it comes to establishing Child IRAs for their children. There are many more options for those with family-owned businesses, allowing them to pay their children at much younger ages. "I thought of doing this for my child based upon my own research and understanding of taxes and financial planning. I worked at a very large CPA firm and then a small two partner firm before going out on my own and the 'kids on the payroll' was a popular tax strategy we used when appropriate. I guess I learned from – and was taught by – senior partners and I saw the benefit to the client and the client's child."

Starting his own firm provided Lumby with the opportunity to start a Child IRA for his oldest offspring. "My son was five years old when I setup the IRA for him," he says. "I've only used the strategy for one year when I used his images in some marketing materials. The total pay and amount deposited in the Roth was just $200. Again, I take seriously the idea that the pay to the child needs to be a fair arm's length transaction. I don't want to get audited and have to reverse everything and pay fines or penalties. My research indicated that somewhere around $200 would be fair for the modeling work he provided. I documented that research in my own tax file to save just in case. Obviously as he grows and is able to perform more work-related tasks, it will make sense to give him more responsibility and pay. But it would be very hard to justify that a 5-year old provides ongoing services for our businesses. He does like to eat all the chocolate in the waiting area, but I don't think that would qualify."

While opportunities abound, risks exist, too. "Obviously, the biggest challenge (and potential audit issue) is getting the child earned income," says Lumby. "The tendency for business owners is to overpay their children for simple tasks. This is a mistake and a huge audit risk. You need to pay your child a legitimate wage for the work they do. For example, if you have professional photos taken of your child to use in marketing materials, you need to call around and see the going rate for what these child shoots would be. So, if a typical photo shoot for a child model would pay $300 in your area, it would be very unwise to pay your child $3,000 for this task. In summary, it is fine to pay your child for legitimate work to do, but you need to pay fair market wages for those tasks. I personally used my son in some marketing materials and paid him a few hundred bucks that we then put into a Roth IRA for him."

So, what does Gabe's son think about all this? "My son is just 5 years old, so he has no idea about the Roth IRA," says Lumby. "Because of his young age, I haven't really thought too much about discussing the Roth

IRA with my son. I guess I just planned on telling him as I'm able to teach him about financial topics, but I'm sure that will be quite a few years down the road. I've thought about the fact that my son could turn out to be a real pain in the rear and I may not want to provide him these financial benefits, but I don't worry too much about it. If that is the case, I might kick myself in a decade. Ha ha."

*　　*　　*　　*　　*

In 2016, a study found 1.2 million husband and wife teams like Jacob and Vanessa Lumby running their own businesses.[1] This represents only a portion of family-owned businesses. According to data compiled on 2007 tax returns, in that year a total of 23.1 million people filed as sole proprietors, of which 16.9 million were profitable.[2] These numbers do not include farms, partnerships, and corporations. A 2003 study, based on estimates in previous research, assumed 60% of all partnerships and corporations can be defined as "family-owned," and calculated a total of 24.2 million family businesses in the United States.[3]

And yet, save for a very few forward-thinking parents and financial service providers like Gabe Lumby, you just don't see a prevalence of Child IRAs these numbers might suggest should exist. Most of the focus on Child IRAs, it seems, concentrates on teenage workers. This makes sense. For one thing, most children can't start earning income (a necessary prerequisite to contributing to a Child IRA) until they reach the age of 14. As a result, many financial firms see minors aged 14 and above as a much more lucrative market. (It turns out, this may offer an opportunity for savvy financial professionals, but more on that in the next chapter.)

Parents (and sometimes even grandparents) who own their own businesses don't have to wait until their children turn 14 "because a business owner can place a child on the payroll to qualify for IRAs," says Timothy Shanahan. "My own children worked part time for my firm starting in elementary school. I used a number of techniques to optimize our tax/investment situation including Roth IRAs which were intended initially for college tuition but I was able to pay for college without touching them so now my children have accounts worth over $50k each."

With roughly 20 million family-owned businesses, there's a huge untapped opportunity for many children to begin their journey towards a multi-million dollar retirement. This journey begins with these three steps:

Step #1: Does Your Business and Do Your Child's Earnings Qualify

As we learned in Chapter 18, children generally cannot work until age 14. There's an important exemption that parents of family-owned businesses can take advantage of. If you own your own business, federal labor laws allow you to hire your own child – in most cases. You can't ask your children to work for you if it's a hazardous or dangerous job. You also can't require your children to work during hours they would normally be required to go to school. Additionally, state labor laws may be more restrictive than federal child labor laws, in which case the parent must abide by the higher standard.

Things can get dicey at the state level. Here's an example. In 1955, Frederick and Rosemary Nuzzo started a pizzeria in New Haven, Connecticut. When they retired they passed multiple locations to their sons. One of their sons, Michael, decided to prepare his young children (ages 13, 11, and 8) to eventually inherit the business. So he placed his oldest son in the kitchen, where he learned from his father how to make pizza. His younger son and daughter worked in the front helping their mother clear tables. When a patron complained about "child labor," Connecticut authorities came to the restaurant, found the children were working there, and cited Michael and his wife for child labor violations as Connecticut law prohibits children below the age of 14 from working. The parents sued (and garnered national press).[4] The suit was eventually settled with "everybody happy."[5] While it wasn't reported whether the children were allowed to continue working in the family business, three years later Nuzzo's pizzeria was named the "Best Thin Crust New Haven Style Pizza,"[6] and a picture from the same year under the heading "Best Pizza Place" in the annual "Best of New Haven" contest showed both Michael and his son.[7]

Needless to say, it's always best to consult a labor law attorney before hiring your children, no matter what their age.

Although most family owned businesses are sole proprietorships based out of the home with no other employees, many are larger firms that employee non-family workers. This poses some important questions. Steven J. Weil, describes them as: "Can I remember to treat my child like any other employee and expect them to be productive, follow the rules, and be on time so that they learn good work skills? Am I paying my child an amount equal to what I would have to pay someone I was not related to for the same work?"

It goes without saying children must remain subject to existing employee rules and regulations. The subject of pay, however, presents a more contentious issue for parent businesses both with and without non-family workers. There are some aspects of normal workers that do not apply to your children. "Many parents enjoy hiring their children to help in the family business," says Bonnie Lee, owner of Taxpertise in Sonoma, California. "It's good training for the day when they will take over. However, there are some who use this merely as a write-off and it's here that the IRS attempts to sniff out fraud. Well, maybe fraud is too strong a word because it's not like the miscreant will go to jail. But if you provide the kid a W2 so you can get the tax deduction and no services were provided by the child, the IRS will disallow the deduction. They want to see timesheets, paystubs, anything to prove the kid did the job. Absent those items, the deduction is taken away. But if an employer hires his child as a bona fide employee, he does not have to withhold and match Social Security, Medicare, or Federal Unemployment Tax (FUTA), that's only if it's your own child and the child is under age 18."

Saving money on payroll taxes is a good thing. The actual payroll number may present a challenge, particularly if the position is unique and there are no other comparable positions already on staff. In most cases, what you pay your child needs to pass the smell test. "Generally, income is considered in return for work," says Scott Vance. "For a child working in a family business, in my tax practice, I would expect a common-sense approach with some supporting documentation. For instance, I wouldn't expect a 12-year-old kid to provide legal services in a family law firm and billing at a rate of $200 an hour. I would look to see that the child's age, type of work performed, and amount paid to the child are comparable."

As a rule of thumb, you might want to start with the prevailing minimum wage, and work the hourly rate up as the required skills increase. Weil says, "The amount paid should not exceed what you would pay a non-related party to perform the same work. For example, putting merchandise back on shelves does not require any special skill. Thus, minimum wage might be right in that case. A teen with web design skills at $25.00 an hour could be a bargain."

Step #2: Choose a "Best-Fit" Job for Your Child

Once you decide your business can hire your child, you'll quickly find out how easy it is as a business owner to bring your child on board. Why is it so effortless? "It's easy because parents can dictate the job description for their child and the duties in order to be able to have earned income," says Jenkin.

This works both ways. "If the parents own their own business, it makes it easier for the child as they don't have to go out there and get a job," says Marianela Collado. Of course, older children might realize this advantage, but younger children might be missing out on good lessons if they think everything will be handed to them. But this is a problem with all endeavors that involve helping your children. At some point, they have to learn to help themselves. But that's the subject of another book, not this one.

Chapter 19 talked about jobs for children based on school age. That chapter discussed those jobs in a theoretical sense. This chapter presents some actual cases and the real jobs undertaken by children for their parents' businesses. Lumby works with small family-owned businesses who have hired their own children. Here are some examples of actual work he's helped business owners implement with their children:

- Advertising marketing materials for their business (mentioned above)
- Cleaning the business office space
- Doing general office duties (putting stamps on mail, checking the PO Box, filing duties, light computer admin work, etc...)
- Mowing the lawn at the commercial office

Lumby likes to advise his small business clients to establish Child IRAs for their child-employees. "Really, any job that you would pay someone else to do that the child can perform is an opportunity for earnings to then contribute to a Roth IRA," says Lumby. "The child will benefit from the time value of money/compounding interest. Plus, if the vehicle used is a Roth IRA, they will likely never pay tax on the initial deposit nor the earnings nor the distributions. It is like free money! There really isn't a better opportunity to set your child up for future success/retirement than getting started as soon as possible with a Roth IRA if they have legitimate earned income to use to contribute."

So, then, how exactly do parents go about hiring their children? We saw earlier in this chapter how Lumby did it for his own 5-year old son. In previous chapters we saw other case studies of parents who hired their children and the kinds of jobs they tasked their children to perform. Lumby tells us of two other circumstances for a couple of very typical family-owned businesses:

The Professional Service Firm Administrative Assistant:

Like Lumby himself, many parents' businesses are professional offices. Professional offices need – you guessed it – professional office workers. This includes a wide variety of jobs most children can perform. Lumby tells us of one of his clients who also provides professional services. "His 15-year old daughter provides administrative services to him for around 10 hours a week. She does anything and everything that a typical administrative professional would do including returning phone calls, maintaining a filing system, setting appointments, checking email, etc. He pays her $10/hr which is a competitive wage for our area. He should have no issues as everything has been well documented. This amount of work and pay allows her to completely fill up her Roth IRA each year."

The Rental Property Landscaper:

As we saw earlier with Rodney Davis, it's not unusual for parents to own rental property. While not their main job, they often create side businesses to manage and operate the property. You don't have to be an expert handyman like Rodney in order to employ your children. There are much more manageable (and traditional) home-related jobs kids can do. Lumby says, "We have a client who has a few teenage boys and owns a bunch of single family rental properties. Instead of paying a lawn care company, they pay their sons to do the mowing each week (they don't like trusting the tenant to maintain the property). He called up a few local lawn care companies to get competitive bids for all the properties. He pays his sons the average of the two bids received. This work doesn't provide enough income for each son to max out the Roth for each of them, but it does provide a few thousand dollars each year for each of them to contribute to their Roth IRAs."

Step #3: Open That Child IRA and Start Your Child on the Road to Becoming a Multi-Millionaire in Retirement

We won't repeat here what we've said several times earlier about the mechanics of creating and contributing to a Child IRA. Rather, we'll focus on a couple of different twists that pertain to parents and grandparents who own businesses.

If You Like the Child IRA, Just Imagine the Power of the Child 401k

Sure, parents can set up Child IRAs for their children-employees. But those aren't the only retirement plans available to business owners. Small business owners regularly use retirement savings vehicles for themselves, and there's no reason why they can't use them for their children, too (just like they would use them for any other employee).

Two of the more popular plans are the SEP-IRA and the more familiar 401k. Each allows for a higher potential contribution (based on the employee's annual earning), but, more important, each permits an employer contribution. It's outside the limited scope of this book (remember, we're talking about "Child IRAs" here, not "Child SEP-IRAs" or "Child-401ks"), so you'll need to talk to your tax consultant to explore the ramifications of these vehicles. If you want to tease yourself on the possibilities, check out Appendix IV – A Turbo-Charged Child IRA – The Child Solo 401k. This might just blow your mind, especially if your child hits a gold mine like some of the case studies we examined in earlier chapters.

A Special Situation: The Grandparent Owned Business

For the most part, this chapter speaks only of the child labor exemption allowed for parents hiring their minor children. It's not evident how this applies to grandparents, although a case can clearly be made the exemption is more likely to apply if the grandparents have legal custody of the children. While each situation has its own set of different circumstances, for our case let's assume the grandparents aren't allowed the child labor exemption. First, grandparents always have the option of gifting an amount equal to earned income that will be contributed to the Child IRA (although this still requires the child to earn that income from some outside source). Second, in the special case of a grandparent-owned business, it's possible there may be creative ways to stay within the letter of child labor laws and still have the grandparent's business pay for the grandchild to work. As in all cases, it's important to check with tax and legal advisors to insure compliance.

In the end, it makes sense for parents who own businesses to hire their children. Weil says, "Paying your child does two things: 1) it gets money out of your tax bracket and into theirs (the first $6,350 they earn is tax free), and 2) it teaches them important life skills and about money and its value."

If this makes so much sense, why aren't more family-owned businesses using this tax saving technique that also allows their children to save for retirement through a Child IRA? Perhaps it's because they simply don't know. How would they discover this advantageous financial tactic? Obviously, they could read this book. More likely, though, they'd go to the resource that answers most of their tax and financial questions. That's the people who must read Appendix V.

What could be done for the rest of us? How can we broaden the availability of the Child IRA to everyone, not just to children who earn income? The next chapter explains how this can easily be accomplished.

CHAPTER TWENTY-FIVE: FOR THE REST OF US

You've made it to this chapter. That could only mean one thing. Well, three things. You want to know what happens if: a) The parents of the child don't own their own business; b) The child can't earn income; or, c) The child needs that income to live and the parents/grandparents don't have the money to gift to the child to offset that earned income and contribute to a Child IRA.

In all three cases, the bottom-line is this: The child is unable to establish a Child IRA. That means the child won't get a head start on their retirement savings. That means the child won't have the opportunity to increase the chances of retiring in comfort. That means the child will have no choice but to confront the challenge of saving for retirement in the same way earlier generations have had to.

Before we dive too far into this, we must recognize, even when opportunities become available, people simply opt out of saving for retirement. A recent study tells us 38% of the employees who have a 401k option do not participate.[1] We therefore are forced to accept that opportunity alone cannot compel people to save for retirement.

That being said, not everyone needs to save for retirement. Some possess so much wealth that tax deferred retirement saving offers no appreciable value. On the other end of the spectrum, some maintain a lifestyle so frugal there's no need to save for retirement as Social Security or some other pension system provides all that is needed.

Still, this truth remains: Unless and until we return to the family-based retirement model of nineteenth century pre-industrial revolution America, most people need to save for retirement. We must encourage retirement saving. To accomplish this, we need to continue to provide a variety of savings vehicles.

The main obstacle to establishing a Child IRA is the requirement to earn income. Even with earned income, as the third point in the opening paragraph alludes to, not all people can afford to save. Don't assume this applies only to low income families. Nearly one in three people earning between $50,000 and $99,999 are living paycheck-to-paycheck.[2] It might astonish you to find out that same survey reveals one in ten people making over $100,000 live paycheck-to-paycheck.[3]

Teaching people to live within their means is important, but this book wasn't written to address that. The objective of *From Cradle to Retirement* is to show people how they can better prepare their children and grandchildren to live a comfortable retirement. Current laws permit only some people to achieve this goal.

There are those who complain it's not fair that only some can benefit from the Child IRA. That's true. Everyone should have that same opportunity. At the same time, we need to urge those who can to take advantage of a Child IRA, there's nothing wrong with brainstorming ways to make the Child IRA more accessible. Let's review three such strategies.

Strategy #1: The Hard Way
Encourage More Family-Owned Businesses

In a sense, this is a return to Early America. For most of our country's first century, small family owned and operated businesses dotted the landscape. With the onset of industrialization, competitive pressures required capital investment beyond the abilities of most families. This persisted through the end of the twentieth century. Things may be changing. According to the *Harvard Business Review,* "In the context of competition in the 21st century, family businesses have innate strengths over other forms of ownership, especially public companies.[4] The tax reform bill of 2017 reflects a broader government effort to encourage private business formation that will likely spur further growth in the number of family-owned businesses.

Obviously, a parent owned business represents the easiest way for someone to allow their child to establish a Child IRA. The child need not impress an employer to get hired. Children working for their parents may enjoy certain tax advantages. In many cases, there's no minimum age requirement.

So, why do I call this strategy "The Hard Way"? For one thing, it requires the parents to set up a business. That's not easy. Not everyone has the interest, inclination, or intuitive sense to create and operate a profitable business. Even if they do, if they happen to live in the wrong state (see our Connecticut pizzeria owner in Chapter 14) their children might be prohibited from working. To rectify this incongruity in state child labor laws, all states must adopt a uniform child labor law allowing family businesses may hire their own children, regardless of age, as long as the work environment is safe, and the occupation not considered dangerous.

Strategy #2: The Harder Way
The Federal Government Passes a "Child IRA" Law

Under the current IRA law, one must have earned income in order to contribute to an IRA. This discriminates against those children who don't have the opportunity to earn income. To change this would require a change in the existing tax code. After going through the 2017 tax reform legislation, most would consider this strategy "harder" than the first strategy.

How might the tax code be changed. There's a number of ways to do it. Here's one idea.

Regarding the maximum contribution, it would be the same as with regular IRAs ($5,500). This cap would apply to the individual Child IRA, not on how much anyone can contribute. For example, grandparents can contribute, say, $1,000 per grandchild per year for each of their 15 grandchildren as long as no individual grandchild's Child IRA received more than $4,500 from all other sources. The grandparents would have contributed a total of $15,000 to fifteen different Child IRAs. That's well above the $5,500 cap on individual IRAs.

The Child IRA would be available in both the Roth and the traditional (tax deductible) version. Budget bean counters might show concern regarding the "revenue neutrality" implications of creating a Child IRA law. Unfortunately, their ironic counting methods overweight the short-term and underweight the long-term impact. Based on recent discussions, it would appear policy wonks prefer the Roth version as it would lead to no immediate revenue losses. Of course, since Roth IRAs are taxed upfront, unlike traditional (tax deductible) IRAs, they don't generate taxes when withdrawals are made. This results in long-term revenue losses (as IRA money which would normally be taxed will not be taxed as it is in a Roth IRA). On the bright side, these long-term term revenue losses could be offset by a reduction in Social Security eligibility (initially with high earners) phased in during future years. Conversely, the traditional (tax deductible) IRAs would produce short-term revenue losses which would be more than offset by long-term revenue gains. Whether this requires an offset depends on which politician is doing the accounting. Those using static models will feel the short-term "loss" will need to be offset. Those using dynamic models may feel future taxes will need to be cut in order to make the model "revenue neutral."

Strategy #3: The Easier Way
Expand the Definition of 529 Plans

In 1986 Michigan Governor James J. Blanchard decided residents of the Great Lakes State needed help saving for college; thus, the Michigan Education Prepaid Tuition Plan (MET) was created. This became the nation's first 529 plan (although Section 529 wasn't added to the tax code until 1996). A 529 college savings plan allows, for the most part, nearly anyone to contribute almost anything to an account dedicated to paying education costs. While blessed at the federal level, each state is responsible for offering its own 529 plan. Contributions may be tax deductible at the state level but aren't at the federal level. Withdrawals are not taxable as long as they are for an educational purpose.

What if states began amending their 529 plan laws to add "retirement" withdrawals (say, those taken after a certain age) to the list of approved withdrawals? This would have the same effect as creating a

Child IRA, only without the earned income requirement and without the contribution caps. You'd still have to pay federal taxes, but, hey, if enough states get on board, the federal government might just be pressured into amending its Section 529. This is exactly how we got Section 529 in the first place. So many states had created college savings programs that the federal government was virtually forced to respond by creating Section 529. It didn't have a choice.

Consider the possibilities that come from using the 529 plan framework as a method to save for retirement. Any person can contribute to any 529 plan, although that contribution shouldn't be more than the annual gift tax exclusion. In 2018, the annual gift tax exclusion is $15,000. Any one person can't gift more than $15,000 to any other person (but givers can gift $15,000 to as many people as they want). The annual gift tax exclusion applies to individual givers, not to couples. So, if you've got four grandparents, each can give you $15,000 a year for a total of $60,000. Not bad for just being born.

With this in mind, it's not hard to image a modified 529 plan becoming a turbo-charged retirement savings vehicle. It might not be the perfect solution to starting a Child IRA, but it will make Child IRAs more accessible to a greater number of people.

So which state will step forward to be the first?

*   *   *   *   *

Dictionary.com defines "self-sufficiency" as the ability "to supply one's own or its own needs without external assistance."[5] The Child IRA offers to bring a new generation of Americans closer to financial self-sufficiency during their retirement years. In the process of doing so, it will require the generation to become financially literate at an earlier age, develop an entrepreneurial spirit, and embrace the wisdom of the broader community they ultimately must serve. In doing this, they'll discover ways to rely less on the government and more on themselves and their economic environment. As they become self-sufficient, society will find itself less burdened. Collectively, then, we will be able to focus more of our attention to activities that can improve ourselves as a neighborhood, as a nation, indeed, as a world.

Section Six:

– Appendices –

Bonus Materials for those Who Desire to Gain a Bit of an Edge

Appendix I.
The Child IRA – FAQ

The idea behind Child IRA as discussed within the context of this book first appeared in the article "What Every 401k Plan Sponsor and Fiduciary Should Disclose to Employees: How to Retire a Millionaire (Hint: It's Easier Than You Think)," (*FiduciaryNews.com*, February 25, 2014). A spreadsheet accident led to a follow-up article, the first to mention the phrase "The Child IRA." The almost penicillin-like serendipity led to the publication of the article "This idea will solve the retirement crisis, guaranteed!?" (*BenefitsPro*, February 26, 2014). It quickly became apparent The Child IRA could easily obviate the need for Social Security. This led to the article "It's time we create a Child IRA," (*Benefit Selling*, April 2014). Finally, the entire notion of The Child IRA was fleshed out and repurposed to become Appendix V in the book *Hey! What's My Number? – How to Improve The Odds You Will Retire in Comfort*, (Christopher Carosa, 2014, Pandamensional Solutions).

Since then, and especially given the publicity with the launch of From Cradle to Retirement's Kickstarter campaign, we've seen plenty of excellent questions about how The Child IRA works. We've distilled the most popular questions here.

Question #1: I like it! The Child IRA is a tremendous way for me to introduce a valuable tool to my clients. I do wonder, however, if it's a good idea to "guarantee" a person's retirement. In some ways worrying about our futures make us better as it's an incentive to become more engaged in our careers and engagement is healthy. How would the Child IRA impact a person's ambition?

Answer #1: First, like any other IRA, there are no "guarantees" regarding what the future might look like, there are only probabilities. The calculations assume an average growth rate of 8% – which is 3% below the historical average growth of 11% a year (that's enough to account for inflation, fees, and whatever else you want to account for).

Then there's this mathematical reality: The $2.5 million 70 years from now merely replaces Social Security – the child will still need to save for retirement as an adult in order to secure a comfortable retirement. If that doesn't answer the "ambition" question, consider this. There's this behavioral trick bartenders do to encourage tips: They always place a few dollars in the "Tip Jar" before the customers arrive. Seeing money already in there encourages patrons to add to the kitty. Think of this Child IRA as the "Tip Jar." Once the child sees the money accumulating year after year, it is likely to trigger a behavioral response consistent with bar patrons: They'll be more likely to save more!

Question #2: I also wonder if people would be more apt to tap into funds that they didn't save themselves?

Answer #2: Oddly enough, the *From Cradle to Retirement* contains interviews with quite a few "children" who are now adults and whose parents established IRAs for them. Most of them seem to value the "lesson learned" and are even interested in starting Child IRAs for their children. One person, who had a Roth instead of a traditional IRA, did use some of the money to pay for graduate school. This is the issue with using Roths, but not with using traditional IRAs, since the Roths allow for non-penalty withdrawals for education. In both cases, withdrawals normally aren't allowed until age 59½.

Question #3: If parents learn that their children did use the money for frivolous purchases, how would they react and what impact would this have on the relationship they have with their children (i.e., "I can't believe little Billy spent his retirement on a Corvette, what a jerk!")?

Answer #3: As mentioned, money from IRAs cannot be withdrawn without penalty until age 59½ (except in the case of the Roth and that's for the sole purpose of funding education expenses). That doesn't mean you can't take the money out before hand, it just means there's a significant disincentive for premature withdrawals. Still, that's better than no disincentives, which often occurs with Custodian Trusts established for children. For the most part, these trusts are releases "no strings attached" once the beneficiary reaches early adulthood. There is an alternative which still uses the IRA vehicle. This involves either parent establishing an IRA (most likely a Roth) in their name and listing the child as a beneficiary. This way, the only way the child gets the money is if the parent dies. At least then the parent won't have to suffer to see how the money is squandered. ☺

Question #4: I watched the video on the Child IRA. It's a great concept, but a child can't open an IRA unless they have earned income. The video talks about putting money into a Child IRA at birth through age 19, but the child normally can't work until age 16 and receive a W2 in order to contribute to an IRA or a Roth IRA. Can you give me a little more detail on how that concept is to work based on that fact?

Answer #4: This is a great question as well as a common misperception. It's perhaps the single greatest reason why we haven't seen many people taking advantage of the Child IRA for their young children. In fact, children below the age of 16 do work and earn income. Yes, babysitting and mowing the neighbor's lawn counts as earned income, but children have real jobs, too. You don't think all those child actors work for free, do you? In addition to certain industries that regularly employ children under the age of 16, family owned business generally have no age restrictions when it comes to employing their own children. *From Cradle to Retirement – The Child IRA – How to start a newborn on the road to comfortable retirement while still in a cozy cradle* explains how to establish a Child IRA today in precise, easy-to-understand (and duplicate), detail through actual real-life case studies, interviews with industry professionals familiar with the ins and outs of hiring children, along with expert guidance from financial professionals versed in the mechanics of establishing Child IRAs.

APPENDIX II.
HOW TO MIMIC THE CHILD IRA –
OLD SCHOOL

As a child, Jack Towarnicky first learned the powers of 2 in 5th grade. "I was immediately enamored with the concept of 'doubling' – 1, 2, 4, 8, 16, 32, 64, 128, 256, 512, 1024, 2048, 4096. That was as far as I could get in rapid fire recitation/memorization in my head. It would pop into my head and I would recite it to myself for no apparent reason. Riding my bike. Sitting on the bench waiting for my turn to bat."

You'd think this trivia could only be used on the student version of *Jeopardy!* Of course, that wasn't a realistic option. Still, kids are creative and, armed with an ounce of trivia, they can create a pound of inspired insight. Jack recalls, "One early use of this information was to refute claims by my fourth-grade classmates (and at least one grade school teacher), that the Indians were fools for selling Manhattan Island for '$24 and trinkets' in 1626. I wondered what $24 would be worth – I guessed maybe a billion dollars (I underestimated, but my classmates thought my claim was outrageous - a billion was real money back in the early 1960's). No one had computers, nor calculators. And, of course, the 'trinkets' themselves would be priceless."

This kind of trivia evolves in compelling ways. Twelve years after his grade school "back-of-the-napkin" calculations, Jack's undergraduate business professor confirmed the true power of the Rule of 72. Simply defined, the "Rule of 72" states that, if you divide the rate of return into 72, the answer is the number of years it takes to double your investment. For example, if your rate of return is 6%, your investment will double in 12 years (72 divided by 6 equals 12). Likewise, if your rate of return is 12%, your investment will double every 6 years (because 72 divided by 12 equals 6).

"So I revisited the Manhattan Island issue," remembers Jack. "I concluded that mostly unimproved land was sold for $22 Billion in

1976 dollars (@ 6%) – equivalent to $188 Billion today! At the time, I joked that the original 'trinkets' would bring an even larger price at auction – all but priceless! In an ignorant, simplistic way, all this became linked in my mind."

When Jack started working, the knowledge of the Rule of 72 came back to haunt him. "I actually first experienced the concept of 'long-term investing' as a series of 1970's regrets – once I started working for wages," says Jack. "My regrets included a lack of personal financial education regarding investments, the lack of easy access to investments (in years prior to the 1980's), and my failure to save anything at an early age. In fact, I had a negative net worth, mostly living payday to payday, until I was 28 years old. My life was pretty good, though. By the time I took my first corporate benefits position in 1979, I emerged from debt and some margin began to appear in my finances. I had completed both a BBA in Business Economics and an MBA (both full time attendance at night) and some margin began to appear in my finances. In 1980, I bought my first new car and I made my first true investment in an employer-sponsored savings plan. But the concept of 'long-term' savings was clarified when I opened an IRA in January 1982 – anticipating 35-40 years of accumulation.   Back in 1981/82, you could get a 30-year CD paying almost 12%. I plugged 12% into the Rule of 72, came up with 6, so $1,000 invested today, tax deferred, would double 10 times in 60 years, $1,000,000 (when I reached age 90)! During my MBA course in Portfolio Management in 1979, my professor had explained to me (and others) how stocks had performed relative to bonds – that a 12% return may have been possible in the years after World War II."

Things changed dramatically once Jack became a father. "When my son was born in 1984," he says, "I recognized that I only had 18 years to prepare for his college expenses. I was then age 32. My own father had died when he was 53 (and I was age 17). So, it was clear aggressive action was needed. But, I also took a step back, and wondered how Andy could avoid that same challenge. What could I do to help my newborn son prepare… for his child… someone who would probably start college 50 or so years in the future."

That same year, current events would reignite Jack's fondness for the Founding Fathers – and one of them in particular. This, in turn, sparked an idea. "I had been a fan of the founding fathers since I was a child," says Jack. "Tom Jefferson and Ben Franklin were top of my list. Most people who truly know me, know I am a Frankophile. Past gifts include books on Ben Franklin, posters, magnets, and even a Ben Franklin action figure – who, when squeezed, spouts famous, trite expressions. While my brother-in-law and sister had introduced me to Ben Franklin's legacy of 'long period' investing on behalf of the cities of Boston and Philadelphia many years earlier, when my brother-in-law Ron showed up in Houston, Texas in 1984 (to cover the Republican National Convention up the road in Dallas), it was right after the birth of my son Andy just two weeks earlier. It reminded me to 'get to work.' We started setting money aside for Andy's college education. Ben Franklin accounts would have to wait."

But not for long. A daughter, Dayle, was born in December 1987. Within those three years, Jack had learned enough of the mechanics of saving to begin saving for his children's future. He says, "I combined the Uniform Gifts to Minors Act opportunity to make modest gifts to my children in 1987 (contributing more for my son as if I had invested $1,000 at his birth in 1984), then invested the money in non-qualified annuities. I took existing savings and moved it into accounts in their name – so that they would be subject to income taxes on the earnings. My goal was to accumulate monies, tax deferred, earning an equity rate of return for a 60-year period of time. I hoped the 10% early withdrawal penalty tax on withdrawals prior to age 59½ would serve as a natural barrier to access. My goal was not to guarantee that they would be middle class millionaires... someday... but, to ensure that they had the opportunity, should history repeat itself."

After establishing these accounts in just non-qualified annuities, Jack invested them in two large cap growth investment mutual funds. The rate of return was mostly consistent with the S&P 500 index. He eventually told his children what he had done. "When they were teens, I shared the concept," says Jack. "I don't remember either of them having a significant reaction – as I expressed it as becoming a millionaire, maybe 50 years from now. And, then, immediately, I followed it with a comment that, in 50 years, a million dollars might only buy a loaf of bread."

The story doesn't end there. Remember, Jack's initial goal was to fund his children's education. In the back of his mind, he also wanted to take advantage of the "Ben Franklin" concept. He used that same grade school ingenuity to accomplish both objectives. "In 2006, I 'borrowed' almost all of the money to finance college expenses – exposing my children to a 0% income tax rate and a 10% early withdrawal penalty tax on accumulated earnings," says Jack. "I used the money to finance their college expenses. A number of years later, once I accumulated Roth IRA assets in my own name, I 'shifted' their 'Ben Franklin' accounts to a Roth IRA basis. I did this by creating separate IRAs through transfers and naming them as beneficiaries. So, as I am now over age 59½ and the monies have been in Roth IRA accounts for over five years, it now accumulates not only tax deferred but tax free. As a result, if the past repeats itself, and the current tax rules don't change, they may become tax-free middle-class millionaires… someday."

Today, Jack's kids are 33 and 30 years old. If anything, their father's actions have inspired similar savings behavior on their part. "They have a long way to go," says Jack. "No one is guaranteeing 12% returns these days. As I said, though, if history repeats itself, they will be millionaires, someday. That someday is likely to be long after I am dead and gone. Each has consistently funded their own Roth IRAs as well as their Health Savings Accounts – both to the maximum permissible level. I am hoping they will take similar action for their children – should either of them ever marry and have children. Just as important, if I am lucky enough for them to have children in my lifetime, I plan to start Ben Franklin accounts for my grandchildren as well."

In effect, without using any of the strategies mentioned in this book, Jack has been able to mimic the Child IRA using "Old School" methods. "While we did not start with Child IRAs on a Roth basis, today, both effectively have a Roth IRA as if it was established at birth, a family legacy," says Jack. "Should I die before their Roth IRAs reach $1MM, they will be in the enviable position of using distributions based on the inherited IRA rules to fund future Roth IRA contributions, to their own accounts and those of their children – perhaps passing along a family legacy of their own."

Jack is currently Executive Director of Plan Sponsor Council of America. He lives in Westerville, Ohio with his wife Debbie. His two children, Andy and Dayle, live in Martinez, California and New York City, New York.

APPENDIX III.
USE YOUR 401K TO MIMIC THE CHILD IRA

There isn't really any age triggers that determine when employees should consider using their company retirement plan as an intergenerational wealth transfer tool. All plan participants must, from the very beginning, be aware of who their designated beneficiaries are. In most states, the spouse is the default beneficiary, so if the employee wants to designate children or grandchildren, that needs to be proactively done. Furthermore, some states may nonetheless require spouses to agree in writing (a notarized signature is often required) that plan assets will bypass them.

If age isn't the guiding parameter, then some combination of net worth, retirement expense projections, and stage of life (which can be different than age), offer better signposts to be on the lookout for. If, between one's net worth and retirement expense projections, it appears there will be little need to use some portion of retirement savings, that portion can then be earmarked for intergenerational wealth transfer. Additionally, as employees move into the retirement stage of their lives, certain precautionary moves can be taken in anticipation of possibly transferring their retirement savings to succeeding generations.

We can break down the "how-to" portion of this into two segments: set-up and distribution. In the set-up phase, we need to determine which type of account to use and who the beneficiaries should be. We've already determined, given the choice, a Roth 401k is the best option. However, employees may feel the need to use the entire maximum contribution available ($18,000 plus an additional $6,000 if they are 50 or older) for their own retirement savings. They're willing to contribute more, but the caps limit them.

Or do they?

In plans that allow it, employees can go above this $18,000 annual limit by opening up a "Deemed IRA." This allows employees to save an additional $5,500 (or $6,500 if over 50) in either a tax-deferred vehicle or a Roth vehicle. If employees wish to keep the traditional 401k accounts assigned to their personal retirement, then the Deemed IRA can be assigned the role of the "Child IRA."

Once we've determined which type of account we'll be using to mimic the role of the Child IRA, the next step is to identify the beneficiaries. While the spouse is generally the default primary beneficiary, the employee can name secondary and tertiary beneficiaries (e.g., "all children" and "all grandchildren"). The naming of the beneficiaries needs to be done carefully as we shall see in a moment. Before we get to that, though, we need to remind you of a potential hurdle. Some plans and some custodians may have limitations (or, at least, specific non-standard procedures) when a minor child is named as a beneficiary. This is because IRAs for minor children generally can only be established as "custodial" IRAs, whereby some named parent or guardian is responsible for the IRA until the child becomes an adult. This becomes relevant once the original owner of the retirement account passes away and the assets get distributed to the heirs. In many cases, the children may be all adults at this time, but the grandchildren may not be.

Distribution presents its own series of hurdles and compromises. This is where using a parents'/grandparents' retirement vehicle to act as a virtual Child IRA begins to deviate from the pure path. Prior to distribution, the retirement plan account will grow and accumulate wealth just like a Child IRA. Upon the death of the owner, things change.

The original Roth 401k retirement plan account by this time has been rolled over into a Roth IRA. Upon the death of the owner, the Roth IRA becomes an Inherited IRA. The account still grows tax-free and distributions also remain tax-free, but RMDs must be taken out. (Actually, the heir is given a choice between lifetime RMDs and taking the whole account in one lump sum.) The RMDs are based on the life of the beneficiary. Here's where the Inherited IRA differs from the Child IRA – the Child IRA's assets can remain undistributed until the child is retired; the Inherited IRA's assets are distributed annually based on the RMD beginning within a year after the death of the original owner no matter the age of the beneficiary.

By the way, in the case of an Inherited IRA with several listed beneficiaries, the RMD is based on the life of the oldest beneficiary. This hurts the younger beneficiaries. There are ways to avoid this. The original owner can engage an estate planning attorney and have the IRA be split into individual trusts, one for each beneficiary.

Further complicating matters, passing wealth to grandchildren may invoke generation-skipping penalties if the parents of those grandchildren are still alive. This is why owners keep things simple by just naming "all children" as the beneficiary. If there is a desire to skip a generation, it's best to consult with an estate planning attorney familiar with both federal rules and rules within the state you reside.

Hypothetical Example

John Doe became a dad again at age 45. He and his wife Jane had steady jobs and they lived modesty. This allowed them to begin saving for retirement at a very young age. Even at 45, they knew they were projected to accumulate more in retirement savings than they needed. John's company plan allowed him to save in a Roth 401k account. John and Jane decided John would use this to save money for their new son Eddie. John set up a Roth 401k account with Jane as the primary beneficiary and Eddie as the secondary beneficiary.

John and Jane were able to retire at 60. Upon retirement, John immediately rolled over his Roth 401k account into a Roth IRA and named Eddie as the primary beneficiary. Jane had her signature notarized to indicate she approved this rollover.

John and Jane enjoyed retirement. Unfortunately, John passed away at age 75. The Roth IRA was retitled "Eddie Doe Inherited Roth IRA, Beneficiary of John Doe." At the time, the Roth was worth $100,000. Eddie, 30 at the time, decided to take the RMDs rather than the lump-sum option. Based on the IRS RMD tables, (and assuming only a 5 percent growth rate), Eddie received more than half a million dollars in distributions. Eddie, a professional photographer, used the distributions to fund a Child IRA for his newborn girl Crystal.

Beginning the first year she was born, he took pictures of her and used those pictures in his business advertising. He paid Crystal $1,000 each year through his family business. He then placed that $1,000 in a Child IRA he had set up on behalf of Crystal. Eddie had to act as custodian for the account until Crystal turned 18. That was the last year Eddie's company paid her the $1,000 and the last contribution ever made to Crystal's Child IRA. When Crystal retired at age 70, her Child IRA was now worth $2.25 million dollars. She thanked her dad for being so foresighted.

Conclusion:

Corporate retirement plans are designed specifically to allow employees to save for retirement. Traditionally, employees have considered this the sole and exclusive objective of their company's defined contribution plan. Thanks to the Roth 401(option, as well as the Deemed IRA (when available), plan sponsors can now offer the additional benefit of using the retirement plan as an estate planning tool in addition to using it as a retirement savings vehicle. Best, these objectives are not mutually exclusive. Because the accounts remain in the employee's name, they can always be tapped into if retirement projections come up short. Likewise, if the funds exceed retirement objectives, the beneficiary designation automatically transforms the retirement savings account into a wealth transfer vehicle. Because of this broad application, the estate planning ramifications of company retirement plan accounts must be considered by all employees, not just highly compensated workers.

APPENDIX IV.
A TURBO-CHARGED CHILD IRA –
THE CHILD SOLO 401K

The problem with the Child IRA is you have to start it when the baby is newly born (or reasonably thereafter). Are you reading this and thinking, "My children are teenagers, there's no way they can catch up this late in the game." That's not entirely true. Have you ever heard of the "gig" economy? It just may contain the answer.

Remember when you used to hire your kid to do a particularly dirty job you didn't want to do? Let's say an overnight windstorm blew over the trash cans. It's 8 o'clock in the morning. The waste disposal folks come in thirty minutes. You're in your PJs and quite comfortable. You turn to your oldest child and say, "Can you go outside and clean up the garbage? I'll give you five dollars."

Boom! You kid just became a gig worker!

These freelance ventures don't need to be one-and-done. You can hire your child to walk the dog. That's about $10 a week worth of work. It's a regular gig. Now we can get on to more serious things.

Let's switch things around for the moment. Instead of lazing around at home in your pajamas, you're busying yourself at work (pajamas optional, but only on pajama Friday). You've got a few odd jobs that need jobbing. You can hire your kids to do that. They can use that money to fund an IRA. But they'll have to come into the office every day, you'll eat dinner with them every night, and you'll have to bring them along on family vacation. In other words, you'll never get a break from them. And the most they can contribute for retirement is $5,500 a year.

But, what if there was a way to both see your kids less and maybe have them save more for retirement. Rather than bring them on as employees for ongoing tasks, hire them as contractors for short-term projects. Think of the assignments you need done that you might search the internet to find one of those "one-and-done" gig workers. Only don't scan the world wide web. Scan the kitchen table.

There are quite a few brand-building projects most businesses can readily use. We'll review one of them, one that I happen to have recent (and not so recent) experience with: video production.

Thanks to the advent of super-smart phones with extremely user friendly and intuitive software, many of today's teenagers have no problem creating internet-ready videos. Indeed, with the trend towards visual rather than written content, forward thinking business leaders want and need more video content to attract the younger generations (i.e., the markets that are growing).

You can hire a local company or a major media company to make these videos. It'll cost you anywhere from $500 to $10,000. The cost depends on number of cameras used, number of shooting locations, post-production complexity and total time of the video. To give you a sense of how this might vary, I share with you the costs of some video's I had done.

Last summer, I filmed an interview with Ted Benna. It was a two camera straight shoot (meaning nothing was edited out). Post production included cutting back and forth between the two cameras, overlaying the audio (which was on a separate track) and adding an intro and an outro. The total cost was roughly $2,500 for a 30-minute video.

Contrast this cost to what I paid to have a couple of promotional videos done for a book I wrote in 2012. A 60-second book trailer included 4 location shots, one camera, and a separate audio. A 4-minute "sneak preview" video featured a two camera in studio set-up with a separate audio. In the post-production, some animation and several cuts were added. The total cost was roughly $5,000.

Lastly, for this book, I created a Kickstarter campaign that needed a video. I priced out a 90 second animated video and got quotes from $500 to $2,500. I opted to buy the software myself (for $300) and produce the video myself.

Here's the deal. My kids have been able to produce videos like these since high school. I could have hired them on and paid them to produce not one, but several videos. Increasing video content makes whatever you're doing more engaging to your audience.

Imagine your child making twelve one-minute videos a year for your business – one for each month. You'd pay $1,000 for each video, meaning your child would earn $12,000. That's more than twice the allowable deduction in a standard IRA.

There's another vehicle that's perfect for people with extra income when they don't need that extra income to support their current expenses. Think children who are students or adult children with second jobs (i.e., a job working for their parents). It's the Solo 401k plan. "We often see it in a moonlighting situation," says Bruce Gendein. "The extra income from the sole proprietor activities is not needed for life style and the Solo 401k deferrals allows them to save a large part of the business earnings."

Let's return to our not-so-imaginary situation where your child makes videos on the side. What if your child, as a sole proprietor, established a Solo 401k? Then that entire $12,000 could be saved for retirement. "The Solo 401k allows you to defer up to 100% of your income (up to $18,500)," says Patrick Dinan, president of Impact Fiduciary in Los Angeles, California.

The Solo 401k also allows for a Roth option, too. There are, however, a couple of major differences with Solo 401k plans. First, they're only available to businesses where the owner is the sole employee. This makes them perfect for the gig worker. On the downside, there may be more paperwork once the assets in the Solo 401k reaches a certain threshold.

Your child may be too old to fully benefit from a Child IRA, but if you own your own business, there's no reason why your child can't turbo-charge retirement savings by starting a "Child" Solo 401k.

APPENDIX V.
FOR INTERNAL USE ONLY – HOW FINANCIAL PROFESSIONALS CAN CREATE A CHILD IRA BUSINESS MODEL

There's an apocryphal story concerning the oak-timbered roof of Oxford's New College Dining Hall that bears telling, even though it is completely false. Well, sort of.

The tale begins in 1865, when an itinerant bug researcher discovered beetles had been eating away at the esteemed Hall's grand roof. With the cost of replacing the original oaks beyond the budget, administrators grew anxious. One of the undergraduates suggested the Dean contact the Forestry Department to see if they had any oak trees of suitable age. When asked the forest manager answered, "We've been wondering when you'd ask."

The story goes on to reveal the secret behind this statement. They built New College in the fourteenth century. At the same time, they also planted a grove of oak trees. These oak trees had only one purpose. They were to provide the necessary lumbar when it came time to replace the Hall roof centuries later.

While this version is a bit exaggerated, the essence remains faithful to actual history.[1] The College forest did provide the oak trees for the 1865 restoration of the original Hall roof. The morale of this fable speaks loudly to the rewards of planning ahead. Sow your seeds today, and tomorrow an oak tree will provide the roof over your head.

$$* \qquad * \qquad * \qquad * \qquad *$$

Before starting a business, every entrepreneur needs to consider, understand, and embrace either one or several alternative exit strategies. Without an exit strategy, all that hard work spent over a lifetime will amount to nothing more than treading water. That's a lot of energy to end up going nowhere. The reason you determine an exit strategy as the first step before starting your business coincides with planting those oak trees when the New College Dining Hall was built. Success requires forethought. Plan ahead and you will reap rich rewards.

At this point, you might be asking, "What does this have to do with the Child IRA?" For financial service providers, the sum total of their clients represent a vast forest. In a forest, when trees mature, the forester harvests them and plants seedlings to replace them. For financial professionals, when clients "age-out" by harvesting their assets, new clients must be found to replace them.

No doubt some of you see where I'm headed. If it makes sense to replace trees with seedlings, wouldn't it make sense to find the client equivalent of seedlings? That's where the Child IRA comes in. If a financial adviser commits to finding family business owners as clients, the opportunity to cultivate Child IRAs ("seedlings") presents itself. By focusing on the care and maintenance of these Child IRAs, you can simultaneously help wean the next generation off of any dependency on Social Security and grow a business out of nothing. Let me give you an example.

Suppose you start with only five family-owned business clients. (I know, I know, you're saying, "Only five?") Each family has four children for a total of twenty children. If you can help them create Child IRAs (whether from the moment the baby is born or for older children including catch-up contributions as shown in Chart I in Chapter 11), in twenty years, each child will have $50,000 for a total of $1 million. If you stay in business another ten years, each Child IRA will have grown to $120,000 (for a total of $2.4 million). If you began your business at age thirty and plan to retire at age 70, the children of those five families will each have a quarter of a million dollars in their Child IRAs (for a total of $5 million). In other words, those Child IRAs, by themselves, added $5 million to your firm's assets.

It's not unusual for financial professionals to have more than five family business clients. You can easily imagine having ten times (or, if you're really good, twenty times) that amount. If they all average four children, you've just helped 200 (or 400, if you're really good) children live a more comfortable retirement. In addition, you've added $50 million (or $100 million) in assets to your firm. When it comes time to retire (remember, always know your exit strategy before you begin), the value of your business has grown tremendously because you've added Child IRAs to your service array.

I'm sure many of you are shaking your head in disbelief. Growing a business can't be this easy. And can you really do well by doing good? Certainly. You'll feel a sense of "giving back" once you see the Child IRAs, after you've helped birth and nurture them, grow to mature levels. And the children behind those Child IRAs will appreciate the power of compounding in ways you can't even imagine.

But those dollar sizes I spoke of? You're right. They're wrong. They're wrong because they're too conservative. I mean, really, do you think children with Child IRAs will stop saving for retirement once they become adults? No way. If, as I greatly expect, the results of compound growth are as addictive as I think they are, the now adult children will be motivated to save more precisely because they've seen the benefits of their Child IRA. And if they're saving more, they're investing more, and they'll have a greater need for financial advice – your financial advice.

Despite the power behind these numbers, the fact remains most financial professionals shy away from start-up IRAs (which, by definition, include Child IRAs). Why? The reason should be obvious:

- "A 'start-up' IRA would tend to be small in size and not very productive initially as a revenue producer for the adviser," says Timothy Shanahan, CEO, Compass Capital Corporation in Braintree, Massachusetts.
- "New IRA's generally do not generate much compensation to financial advisers," says Jose Silva, Founder & CEO of Silva Fiduciary Advisors in Daytona Beach and Orlando, Florida.
- "There is no financial gain," says Ted Jenkin, co-CEO and Founder of oXYGen Financial in Alpharetta, Georgia.

The fact is, most people never think to plant those oak trees. They're too busy building the Dining Hall. Too many financial professionals fall into this category. "They might shy away because they may not see the long-term benefits of establishing a relationship with the younger generation now and they may view those accounts as 'non-profitable'," says Marianela Collado, CEO and Senior Financial Advisor with Tobias Financial Advisors in Plantation, Florida.

This can mean only one thing: Opportunity, (yes, I spelled it with a capital "O"). If most advisers shun start-up IRAs because they're short-term loss leaders (spoiler alert: they are), that means anyone coming into the market as a Child IRA specialist will face little to no competition. (Admit it, did I have you at the word "little" or the word "no"?)

While it might not yet be the focus of their business, a few forward-thinking professionals mimic Gabe Lumby's strategy. They encourage their clients to established Child IRAs for their offspring. "I have suggested to clients and other financial professionals (I mentor many) about having parents open a Roth IRA for their child," says Andi Wrenn, a financial counselor and marriage coach in Raleigh, North Carolina. "The best part is this: Tax free withdrawals at retirement age. They can contribute up to the limits of what they earn. It doesn't have to be the actual dollars they earn. Parents and grandparents can fund it, but they need to have earned the amount deposited into the account. One client has their son use money he makes mowing and babysitting to be able to participate in this. It can really add up if they start this young."

Some planners see this as a chance to get kids started on the road to financial literacy at a very young age. "We encourage clients to open up Roth IRAs as early as possible for the children," says Lou Cannataro, partner at Cannataro Park Avenue Financial in New York City. "Just imagine if someone did all of this for us! Not only would we have a jumpstart on our planning, but more importantly, the knowledge and wherewithal to not only verbalize our goals at a much younger age in life but also build the competency to actually begin saving first and then spending what's left over!"

Nothing teaches best like doing, and starting a Child IRA is the ultimate in "boots-on-the-ground" training for young and impressionable minds. "It's never too early to start discussing money with your children and encouraging them to begin saving for retirement," says Rachel Gottlieb, a New York-based financial planner and SVP at UBS Wealth Management. "Some of my clients' children, who are under the age of 18, have started contributing to IRAs or Roth IRAs, after they start earning income in their first jobs, or high school jobs. If they don't need that money for spending, it's great to start getting them in the habit of contributing to IRAs."

And who is best to proctor these lessons than a veteran professional. "For many, the reality is our parents did not have the knowledge to discuss financial planning nor the cash flow to start planning for us when we were children," says Cannataro. "However, many of our clients now do have the assets and the knowledge. With a knowledgeable team, it is important to bring the next generation as early as possible to the planning table."

The professionals who are actively promoting Child IRAs use both formal and informal processes to do so. Silva's process is "very simple." He says, "I inquire if they have young children and if so, recommend that they set up an IRA for them. Explain to them that cost is minimal and the value and lessons learned are substantial. I have a few clients with IRA's for their children or grandchildren. It is still a minority of parents that know about this opportunity and less that actually have them set up. If clients have young children, I always talk to them about this as an opportunity to instill good financial habits & values and to appreciate delayed gratification."

For Jenkin, the process begins with teaching fundamental concepts. "When the children get into high school," he says, "we encourage our clients to set up a family meeting so we can teach the kids the basics of budgeting, debt, investing, and saving. This is where we introduce the concept of the Roth IRA and why the child wants to start earning income."

Of course, sometimes parents need a little nudging when it comes to setting up a Child IRA. "Actually, very few parents do this because they don't really understand the rules and IRA's have always been thought of as a vehicle for older people and not younger people," says Jenkin. "We explain early in the process how the time value of money works and why when children have earned income that a Roth IRA or Traditional IRA in some cases makes great sense. There are generally done pro-bono or the children's account is householded into the overall fee for the family accounts."

Some advisers consider the promotion of the Child IRA as something not separate and distinct from their other activities. Collado says, "I don't view this as a 'dedicated service' – we offer holistic wealth management and the service we offer to the parents extends to their children. We encourage all our clients to help their children establish IRAs. Especially when they are minor children who have a summer job. We tell them it is a good way to give their children some financial training wheels and even incentivize them to get summer jobs as parents will 'match' their wages in the form of a Roth IRA contribution."

Others see the Child IRA as something more for adult children. "I have a few clients who have taken our advice to set up Roth IRAs for working age children," says Shanahan. "We help set it up and often fund the child's IRA from the parents account. The process is included with our services and the child's account would enjoy the same fee as the parents."

Still, you'd be amazed how young some of these children are who retirement professionals have helped establish Child IRAs. Jenkin can't recall the exact age, "but I want to say 12 years old. Whenever the children are old enough and qualifies to be on payroll or make earned income we begin introducing the Roth IRA concept."

"I've helped my clients establish Roth IRAs for children as young as 15," says Collado. "In one case, the client's son was mowing lawns and we appropriately suggested that he track his income (and expenses) and then use that 'earned income' for the parents to fund a Roth IRA."

"The youngest child that I set up an IRA for was 10 years old," says Silva. "His name is Antonio. His grandmother, my client, wanted to do something for him educationally and financially so I suggested an IRA.

I explained that she or anyone could pay Antonio for walking the dog, doing yard work, etc. and that amount could be contributed to his IRA. Grandma liked the concept so much that she offered to match any contributions from Antonio. It's been about three years since we started this IRA for them and the balance is currently over $2,000. More importantly, though, Antonio has learned some very valuable new lessons and is very excited about seeing his little pot of money grow!"

As good and helpful financial advisers have been in helping their clients' children start Child IRAs, the effort has brought immediate dividends in return. "It increases the stickiness of our relationship and the overall value we provide to our clients versus firms just seeking to make a sale," says Jenkin.

Since these start-up IRAs don't bring immediate revenues, the Child IRA becomes just another part of the firm's overall value-added proposition. "It is a 'holistic' treatment of the client and may over time start a relationship with the ultimate inheritor of the parent account that we now manage," says Shanahan.

Silva agrees. He says, "It is part of the holistic service approach that I have at my practice. Since we often take care of two or three generations within a family of clients, by offering the IRAs for children we are serving them more comprehensively."

Child IRAs help build lasting bonds between the client and the adviser. "To me it is not so much about helping my business, it is about establishing a relationship with my client's children," says Collado. "My goal is to build a business model that serves families for generations."

The Best Strategy for Building a Child IRA-Based Business for Retirement Professionals

By now, you're thinking of the multiple benefits offered by focusing on Child IRAs. Plus, the relatively little competition in this niche has you asking, "How can I immediately incorporate the Child

IRA to add value and begin building lasting bonds with my clients?" This chapter is long enough, so I'll end with three quick steps.

Step #1: Learn Everything You Can About the Child IRA

While this book is an excellent start, you'll find it most beneficial to have a one-on-one meeting with someone well versed in matters concerning the Child IRA. No two businesses are alike, and, as you know, your business has its own special attributes. It may be where you're physically located, the nature of your clientele, or how you're currently delivering your service. These factors and many others will impact how you can and will incorporate the Child IRA into your practice. Once your comfortable with this step, you're ready to move on to Step Two.

Step #2: Participate in a General Education Session with Your Professional Peers

This can include an internal meeting with your co-workers or during a meeting of your professional association. This offers two primary advantages. First, and ideally, this session is again led by someone intimately familiar with the Child IRA. Second, by being among your peers, you will benefit from their questions, insights, and thoughts. You might not anticipate all the variations that can arise with the Child IRA. Collectively, a group of professionals is more likely to identify most of the main issues. In addition, the comments of others may trigger important questions from you. This session should focus on two critical matters: The specific logistics of establishing a Child IRA and the best methods to use when educating parents (and their children) on the nature and dramatic potential of the Child IRA. When you think it's time to take your show on the road, you may proceed to Step Three.

Step #3: Host a Public Meeting

This meeting can include clients, prospects, or both. It should be clear that you are the facilitator of the event and the "go-to" person for any calls to action. You may discover that offering a featured speaker –

ideally an outside expert on the Child IRA – and not merely someone from your firm, will attract a larger and more engaged audience. In terms of the audience, you'll need to target certain demographic groups. You might consider the advantages of hosting multiple meetings, each designed for a specific niche. For example, you can host a meeting for newlyweds, for expecting parents, for high school students, or for family business owners.

That's it. But remember, the secret to success is often being there first. As of this writing, there aren't many retirement professionals positioning themselves as "Child IRA experts." As this book grows in popularity, you may find a growing crowd of experts, especially if state and federal politicians jump on the Child IRA bandwagon. Far-fetched, you say? Maybe not, as you no doubt found out by reading Chapter 25.

APPENDIX VI.
FOOTNOTES

Foreword
[1] Karl Marx, "History repeats itself, first as tragedy, second as farce"; George Santayana, Those who do not remember the past are condemned to repeat it."; Oscar Wilde, "A pessimist is somebody who complains about the noise when opportunity knocks."; Plato, "Let parents bequeath to their children not riches, but the spirit of reverence."; Campbell Soup Company, "I coulda' had a V-8."

[2] Library of Congress. American Memory. "What is the American Dream?" lesson plan, James Truslow Adams, 1931, Accessed 20170914 at: http://myamerican-dream.org/index.html.

[3] Melody Hopson, President Ariel Investments, 2008; see also Martin Luther King, Jr., in his "Letter from a Birmingham Jail" (1963) he rooted the civil rights movement in the African-American quest for the American Dream. "We will win our freedom because the sacred heritage of our nation and the eternal will of God are embodied in our echoing demands ... when these disinherited children of God sat down at lunch counters they were in reality standing up for what is best in the American dream and for the most sacred values in our Judeo-Christian heritage, thereby bringing our nation back to those great wells of democracy which were dug deep by the founding fathers in their formulation of the Constitution and the Declaration of Independence." Accessed 20170914 at:
http://www.africa.upenn.edu/Articles_Gen/Letter_Birmingham.html.

Chapter 2: A Piece of Ben Franklin's Wisdom You May Not Know
[1] Williams, Edgar, *Inquirer* staff writer, "Franklin's Arrival in Philadelphia," B\August 27, 1980 http://www.ushistory.org/Franklin/essays/franklinarrives.htm.

[2] PBS, Benjamin Franklin, Inquiring Mind, Mesmer, http://www.pbs.org/benfranklin/l3_inquiring_mesmer.html.

[3] WealthyMatters.com, Benjamin Franklin's Gift, January 25, 2011, https://wealthymatters.com/tag/charles-joseph-mathon-de-la-cour/.

[4] The Last Will and Testament of Benjamin Franklin http://www.constitution.org/primarysources/lastwill.html.

[5] Ibid.

[6] Ibid.

[7] George Herbert, *Outlandish Proverbs*, circa 1633

Chapter 3: Ben Franklin's Trusts – Did They Work?
[1] "Philadelphia and Suburbs – City Trusts," *The Philadelphia Inquirer*, Thursday, February 13, 1873, p 25

[2] *The Ogdensburg Advance and St. Lawrence Weekly Democrat*, Thursday, April 4, 1878, p 7

[3] "The Girard Estate – Meeting of the Board of City Trusts and Contract Awarded for New Building," *The Philadelphia Inquirer*, Thursday, September 10, 1885

[4] *The Ogdensburg Advance and St. Lawrence Weekly Democrat*, Thursday, April 4, 1878, p 7

[5] "The Franklin Estate - How It Has Fared In Boston — The Litigation," *The Homerville NY Weekly Tribune*, October 1890

[6] "Ben Franklin Fund Released," *The Philadelphia Inquirer*, Wednesday Morning, March 21, 1962, p 26

[7] *The Naples Record*, Friday, May 13, 1883, p 25

[8] "Board of City Trusts – Much Valuable Information Contained in the Annual Report," *The Philadelphia Inquirer*, Thursday, March 8, 1888

[9] "The Franklin Estate - How It Has Fared In Boston — The Litigation," *The Homerville NY Weekly Tribune*, October 1890

[10] "Art News," *The Evening Post*, New York, Saturday, March 16, 1895

[11] "Franklin's Will in Court," *The New York Times*, September 30, 1890

[12] Ibid.

[13] *The Patterson New Jersey Morning Call*, Monday, July 18, 1892, p.5

[14] Cortland, *New York Standard and Cortland Daily Journal*, Monday Evening, July 18, 1892, p.1

[15] *The Ogdensburg Journal*, Monday, July 18, 1892

[16] "In Doubt Over Franklin's Trust – Can the Boston Trustees Found a Trade School?" *The New York Press*, Wednesday, November 14, 1894

[17] "Court Opinion Asked on Franklin Fund," *The Syracuse Journal*, Tuesday, August 12, 1930

[18] Gill, William, "Boston 'Keeps Politics Out of Franklin Fund'," Long Island Star-Journal, Wednesday, August 8, 1951

[19] "Ben Franklin Fund Released," *The Philadelphia Inquirer*, Wednesday Morning, March 21, 1962, p 26

[20] DeLeon, Clark, "The Scene in Philadelphia and Its Suburbs," *The Philadelphia Inquirer*, February 7, 1993

Chapter 4: The True Legacy of Ben Franklin's Last Will and Testament

[1] Fess, Margaret, "Trust Designed to Act as 'Money Tree'," *Buffalo Courier-Express*, Sunday, March 27, 1960, p 13-B

[2] Ibid., p 13-B

Chapter 5: Ripped from Today's Headlines: The Looming Retirement Crisis

[1] "The Retirement Crisis Is Getting Truly Scary," by Helaine Olen, *Slate*, March 4, 2016

http://www.slate.com/articles/business/the_bills/2016/03/retirement_for_americans_is_getting_even_scarier_the_candidates_need_to.html

[2] Dunn, Peter, "Pete the Planner: Tackling Baby Boomers' retirement crisis," *USA TODAY*, July 22, 2017
https://www.usatoday.com/story/money/personalfinance/2017/07/22/pete-planner-tackling-baby-boomers-retirement-crisis/468473001/

[3] Friedberg, Barbara A., "Are We in a Baby Boomer Retirement Crisis?" *Investopedia*, June 7, 2017
http://www.investopedia.com/articles/personal-finance/032216/are-we-baby-boomer-retirement-crisis.asp

[4] Holodny, Elana, "Larry Fink: There's a big problem with America,s plans for retirement," *Business Insider*, April 10, 2017
http://www.businessinsider.com/larry-fink-on-retirement-crisis-of-living-longer-2017-4?op=1

[5] Ibid.

[[6] Connick, Wendy, "Are We Facing a Retirement Crisis?" *The Motley Fool*, June 17, 2017
https://www.fool.com/investing/2017/06/17/are-we-facing-a-retirement-crisis.aspx]

[[7] Carlson, Ben, "Why Is There a Retirement Crisis?" by *A Wealth of Common Sense*, August 2, 2017
http://awealthofcommonsense.com/2017/08/why-is-there-a-retirement-crisis/]

Chapter 6: American Attitudes on Retirement from the Revolution Through World War I

[1] "The Possible Secret of Our Founding Fathers' Longevity," PAFINDER, January 1995

[2] Exam 1 study guide 3: Colonial America, 1607-1775, © 2017 Quizlet Inc.
https://quizlet.com/112465199/exam-1-study-guide-3-colonial-america-1607-1775-flash-cards/

[3] PAFINDER

[4] PAFINDER

[5] by Fleming, Thomas, "Fleming: What Life Was Like in 1776," Wall Street Journal, July 2, 2012
https://www.wsj.com/articles/SB10001424052702303561504577496620544901322

[6] "A brief history of retirement: It's a modern idea," Seattle Times, December 31, 2013, http://www.seattletimes.com/nation-world/a-brief-history-of-retirement-its-a-modern-idea/

[7] "Mandamus," *The Evening Post* (New York), March 24, 1803

[8] "Fire Department of the City of New-York," *The Evening Post* (New York), January 10, 1804

[9] "By This Day's Southern Mail," *The Evening Post* (New York), January 6, 1802

[10] "An Act," *Buffalo Gazette*, April 14, 1818

[11] Waite, Edward F., "Veteran's Pensions: The Law and Its Administration From the Revolutionary War to the Civil War," Harper's, Volume 86, Issue 512, January, 1893, https://socialwelfare.library.vcu.edu/social-security/veterans-pensions-early-history/

[12] Waite

[13] "Historical Background and Development of Social Security, Extracted on 6/29/17 from Social Security Administration web-site https://www.ssa.gov/history/briefhistory3.html

[14] Waite

[15] Skocpol T. Protecting Soldiers and Mothers: The Political Origins of Social Policy in the United States. Cambridge, MA: The Belknap Press of Harvard University Press; 1992.

[16] "Lemuel Cook Monument," Orleans Republican (Albion, NY) 1900-1906

[17] "Death of Widow of Veteran of 1776," *Duluth News-Tribune* (Duluth, Minnesota), 12 November 1906, page 5

[18] Harrell-Sesniak, Mary, "Last Revolutionary War Widow Receives Final Pension – in 1906!," July 19, 2012 Extracted on 9/4/17 from GenealogyBank web-site https://blog.genealogybank.com/last-revolutionary-war-widow-receives-final-pension-in-1906.html

[19] "Widows of Veterans," *The Duluth Evening Herald*, Tuesday, December 4, 1906

[20] Ibid.

[21] "Confederate widow, 93, dies in Ark.," *The Washington Times*, Monday, August 18, 2008

[22] "Last Civil War widow dies at 97," June 1, 2004, Extracted on 9/4/17 from BBC News web-site http://news.bbc.co.uk/1/hi/world/americas/3765811.stm

[23] Miller, Jennifer, "Last Confederate widow Turns 96," *Enterprise Ledger*, (Enterprise, Alabama), December 8, 2002

[24] "Last Yankee war widow dies," Monday, January 20, 2003, Extracted on 9/4/17 from BBC News web-site http://news.bbc.co.uk/1/hi/world/americas/2677095.stm

Chapter 7: The Rise and Demise of the Corporate Pension

[1] "Falling Short," The Economist, April 7, 2011

[2] Ibid.

[3] McCourt, Steven, Defined Benefit and Defined Contribution Plans: A History, Market Overview and Comparative Analysis, 43 Benefits and Compensation Digest (2006)

[4] Lowenstein, Roger, "The End of Pensions," *The New York Times Magazine*, October 30, 2005

Chapter 8: A Promise Breaking

[1] "President Roosevelt's Own Story of New Deal," Daily Sentinel, Rome, N.Y, Monday Evening, April 25, 1938 (Contained in an authorized advanced publication

of his notes and comments to "The Public Papers and Addresses of Franklin D. Roosevelt.")

[2] Steiner, Sheyna, "Americans racked by retirement fears," Bankrate.com, February 18, 2015

[3] "President Roosevelt's Own Story of New Deal," Daily Sentinel, Rome, N.Y, Monday Evening, April 25, 1938 (Contained in an authorized advanced publication of his notes and comments to "The Public Papers and Addresses of Franklin D. Roosevelt.")

[4] Pettengill, Samuel B., "The Gentlemen From Indiana," *The Knickerbocker News*, Thursday, February 1, 1940

[5] Editorial, *Nassau Daily Review-Star*, Monday, March 20, 1950

[6] Ibid.

Chapter 9: Is This the Solution to the Inevitable Social Security Crisis?

[1] "Historical Average Federal Tax Rates for All Households 1979-2013," Tax Policy Center, Urban Institute and Brookings Institution, 2016, http://www.taxpolicycenter.org/statistics/historical-average-federal-tax-rates-all-households

[2] "Fiscal Year 2014 Budget Overview," Social Security Administration, April 2013

Chapter 16: Not Your Father's IRA – How to Open a New Child IRA for Your Child and Grandchild

[1] "*USA Weekend* calls it quits," *The Davis Enterprise*, December 28, 2014, page A3]

[2] Achibee, Ashley & Beanblossom, Cheryl, "This Mother's Day, think of lifetime financial moves to help kids," *Macoupin County Enquirer-Democrat*, Thursday, May 3, 2012, page 8A]

[3] https://www.fidelity.com/about-fidelity/individual-investing/fidelity-introduces-roth-ira-for-kids]

[4] "Turbocharge your child's retirement with a Roth IRA for Kids," Fidelity Learning Center, https://www.fidelity.com/learning-center/personal-finance/retirement/turbocharge-childs-retirement]

[5] Ibid.

Chapter 18: Child Labor – The Pregnant Pause

[1] "141 Men and Girls Die in Waist Factory Fire; Trapped High Up in Washington Place Building; Street Strewn with Bodies; Piles of Dead Inside," *New York Times*, March 26, 1911, p. 1

[2] "Locked in Factory When Fire Started that Cost 142 Lives," Nassau County Review, March 31, 1911

[3] "Seeking a Place to Blame for Awful Fire Horror," The Pokeepsie Evening Enterprise, March 27, 1911, Page 1

[4] "Cures Girl Victim of Triangle Fire," *The New York Times*, April 8, 1913

[5] "Cures Girl Victim of Triangle Fire," *The New York Times*, April 8, 1913

[6] Beitler, Stu, "New York, NY Triangle Shirtwaist Fire Disaster, Mar 1911," GenDisasters.com http://www.gendisasters.com/new-york/2063/new-york-ny-triangle-shirtwaist-fire-disaster-mar-1911?page=0,1

[7] "Cures Girl Victim of Triangle Fire," *The New York Times*, April 8, 1913

Chapter 24: For Family Owned Businesses

[1] https://www.statisticbrain.com/family-owned-business-statistics/ downloaded August 21, 2017

[2] http://www.fonerbooks.com/taxes/stats.htm downloaded August 21, 2017

[3] Astrachan, J.H. and Shanker, M.C. (2003), "Family Businesses' Contribution to the U.S. Economy: A Closer Look," *Family Enterprise USA*. http://www.familyenterpriseusa.com/wp-content/uploads/2016/09/FB-in-US-2003.pdf downloaded August 21, 2107

[4] "Parents Deny Kids Are Breaking Child Labor Laws By Working At Family's Pizzeria, by Emily Friedman, ABC News, May 28, 2010 http://abcnews.go.com/Business/child-labor-laws-questioned-connecticut-family-pizzeria-lawsuit/story?id=10762561 downloaded August 21, 2017

[5] "Pizza Parents Settle With State," by LeAnne Gendreau, NBC Connecticut, December 10, 2017, https://www.nbcconnecticut.com/news/local/Pizza-Parents-Settle-With-State--111461304.html downloaded August 21, 2017

[6] "Best Thin Crust New Haven Style Pizza Grand Apizza, Clinton," *Shoreline Times*, October 24, 2013

[7] http://www.ctnow.com/best-of/new-haven/local-favorites/ctn-best-of-new-haven-2015-madison-pizza-place-story.html downloaded August 21, 2017

Chapter 25: For the Rest of Us

[1] Barney, Lee, "Nearly 20% of Workers Reduced Their Savings in the Last Year," *PLANADVISER*, August 24, 2017, https://www.planadviser.com/nearly-20-of-workers-reduced-their-savings-in-the-last-year/, retrieved January 28, 2018

[2] Ibid.

[3] Ibid.

[4] Baron, Josh, "Why the 21st Century Will Belong to Family Businesses," Harvard Business Review, March 28, 2016, https://hbr.org/2016/03/why-the-21st-century-will-belong-to-family-businesses, retrieved January 28, 2018 This article states studies show only 30% of family businesses survive past the first generation, 10-15% past the second and 3-5% past the third. The compares to "a study of 25,000 public traded companies from 1950 to 2009 found that, on average, they lasted around 15 years, *or not even through one generation*." Furthermore, the author cites five factors which will only increase the trend towards more family businesses: "Higher Calling," "Captive Capital," "Sustainable Footprint," "Rapid Response," and "Engaged Owners."

[5]self-sufficiency. Dictionary.com. Dictionary.com Unabridged. Random House, Inc. http://www.dictionary.com/browse/self-sufficiency (accessed: January 29, 2018).

Appendix V: For Internal Use Only – How Financial Professionals Can Create a Child IRA Business Model

[1]Prickard, Arthur Octavius (1906). New College, Oxford. London: J.M. Dent, pp 28-30 tells the true story of the Dining Hall roof: "The Hall, the common dining-room, and also the place of meeting for all the more solemn purposes of College procedure, is a noble room eighty feet by forty and very lofty, though the floor is raised high above the level of the Quadrangle. It has been used for successive generations. The fine paneling is associated with one of the most honoured names of the College, having been placed there by Archbishop Warham, when Bursar in the reign of Henry VIII., and was, perhaps, his gift. The marble pavement replaced the original floor in 1722. The open oak roof is of especial interest, both as the first of the more modern works of restoration, and also as a contribution, at least in the first place, made by the junior members of the College. The original roof had been, at the end of the eighteenth century, replaced by a ceiling at the hands of Wyatt, the architect, who has much to answer for; he had to please a generation which preferred comfort to beauty, perhaps we should rather say, which had convenient, though perverted, ideas of the beautiful; we enjoy the comfort and augment it, and we also try to feel our way back to a truer standard of taste; and it has yet to be seen, though the living generation will hardly see it, how posterity will esteem our conscientious efforts. However this may be, the Hall roof was felt to be unworthy of its place. The Junior Common Room, which was practically an independent corporation, comprising the Undergraduates and B.A. Fellow and a few Gentlemen Commoners, its finances varying between opulence and destitution, according as the Steward was an economist like Sydney Smith, or a scatterer, took the first move. An offer of a thousand pounds out of its balance at the time was made to the College, for the purpose of restoring the Hall roof; which, after somewhat prolonged negotiations, was accepted. In 1865 the work was carried out under the care of Sir Gilbert Scott, the great oak beams being all provided out of woods belonging to the College. The result is exceedingly rich and impressive, the lantern in the middle, a work of strict restoration, being especially admirable."
https://archive.org/stream/newcollegeoxfor00pric#page/28/mode/2up

INDEX:

ABOUT THE AUTHOR

Award-winning financial writer Christopher Carosa once exposed the soft underbelly of a trillion-dollar industry (and still has the scars to prove it). Mr. Carosa is a popular and entertaining speaker, appearing from coast to coast. Referred to by his peers as an "imbedded reporter," he has written more than a thousand feature stories, columns, and exclusive interviews as Editor-in-Chief of *FiduciaryNews.com*, contributing weekly columnist for *BenefitsPro*, and regular contributor to a variety of other print and digital news publications.

The author of six books and a popular stage play, Mr. Carosa's widely acclaimed *401(k) Fiduciary Solutions* (Pandamensional Solutions, 2012) has been called "a vital reference tool for years to come." His thoughts and opinions have been sought out by such major media outlets as *The Wall Street Journal, The New York Times, USA Today, Barron's*, CNBC, CNN, and Fox Business News.

A rare breed among financial journalists, Mr. Carosa has accumulated a long, variegated, and successful record as a practitioner in the financial services industry. After earning a degree in physics and astronomy from Yale University in 1982, he joined Manning & Napier Advisers, Inc. During his 14 years there, he helped start the firm's proprietary mutual fund series, created the firm's custodial operations division, and created their trust company that accumulated nearly $1 billion in assets before he left.

Mr. Carosa earned his MBA from the Simon School at the University of Rochester and the CTFA (Certified Trust and Financial Adviser) professional designation from the Institute of Certified Bankers. Today, he is president of Carosa Stanton Asset Management, LLC, a boutique investment firm. He's also Chairman of the Board and President of Bullfinch Fund, Inc. a series of flexible no-load mutual funds, including one that concentrates its investments in Western New York companies.

If you'd like to read more by Mr. Carosa, feel free to browse his author's site, ChrisCarosa.com; LifetimeDreamGuide.com, a site to another book he's working on; his site devoted to his first love, AstronomyTop100.com; and, ChildIRA.com, where both parents and professionals can discover additional bonus material about how to explore the many advantages of The Child IRA.

Mr. Carosa lives in Mendon, NY with his wife, Betsy, three children, Cesidia, Catarina, and Peter, and their beagle, Wally.

Made in the USA
Columbia, SC
17 August 2019